T0323702

Cambridge Elements

Elements in Creativity and Imagination
edited by
Anna Abraham
University of Georgia, USA

PROPHETS AT A TANGENT

How Art Shapes Social Imagination

Geoff Mulgan
University College London

CAMBRIDGE
UNIVERSITY PRESS

CAMBRIDGE
UNIVERSITY PRESS

Shaftesbury Road, Cambridge CB2 8EA, United Kingdom

One Liberty Plaza, 20th Floor, New York, NY 10006, USA

477 Williamstown Road, Port Melbourne, VIC 3207, Australia

314–321, 3rd Floor, Plot 3, Splendor Forum, Jasola District Centre,
New Delhi – 110025, India

103 Penang Road, #05–06/07, Visioncrest Commercial, Singapore 238467

Cambridge University Press is part of Cambridge University Press & Assessment,
a department of the University of Cambridge.

We share the University's mission to contribute to society through the pursuit of
education, learning and research at the highest international levels of excellence.

www.cambridge.org
Information on this title: www.cambridge.org/9781009321655

DOI: 10.1017/9781009321631

First published 2023

A catalogue record for this publication is available from the British Library.

ISBN 978-1-009-32165-5 Paperback
ISSN 2752-3950 (online)
ISSN 2752-3942 (print)

Prophets at a Tangent

How Art Shapes Social Imagination

Elements in Creativity and Imagination

DOI: 10.1017/9781009321631
First published online: January 2023

Geoff Mulgan
University College London

Author for correspondence: Geoff Mulgan, gjmulgan@gmail.com

Abstract: This Element asks if the arts can help us imagine a better future society and economy, without deep social gulfs or ecological harm. It argues that, at their best, the arts open up new ways of seeing and thinking. They can warn and prompt and connect us to a bigger sense of what we could be. But artists have lost their role as gods and prophets, partly as an effect of digital technologies and the ubiquity of artistic production, and partly as an effect of shifting values. Few recent books, films, artworks, or exhibitions have helped us imagine how our world could solve its problems or how it might be better a generation or more from now. This Element argues that artists work best not as prophets of a new society but rather as 'prophets at a tangent'.

Keywords: art, imagination, social, future, technology

ISBNs: 9781009321655 (PB), 9781009321631 (OC)
ISSNs: 2752-3950 (online), 2752-3942 (print)

Contents

Introduction: The Case for Tangential Imagination

This Element is about how art changes our world and our societies. It asks if the arts can help us imagine a better future society and economy, without deep social gulfs or ecological harm, or if they are mainly there to stimulate and entertain but not to transform.

It shows that, at their best, the arts open up new ways of seeing and thinking. They warn and prompt. They connect us to a bigger sense of what we could be, beyond the petty constraints of daily life. Great works of literature, music, film, and painting can crystallise shifting moods of hope, moments when ancient injustices are overturned.

But the role of the arts is not quite what it may seem. Claims that they can blaze a trail for new ways of living, or new ways of organising a society, don't stand up well to scrutiny. Indeed, the arts have never played this role and it is a category error to believe that they could, equivalent to believing that political movements could prompt advances in physics, or vice-versa.

This is even more true today. Artists have lost their role as gods and prophets, partly an effect of digital technologies and the ubiquity of artistic production, and partly an effect of shifting values. The nineteenth century ideal of the tortured genius with unique insights into the future of humanity is an anachronism. Remarkably few recent books, films, artworks, or exhibitions have successfully tried to imagine how our world could solve its problems or how it might be better a generation or more from now. Indeed, parts of the art world now look more like symptoms of the problems than like solutions: ever more integrated with the lives of the ultra-rich, more an emblem of extravagance, waste, and inequality than an answer to the world's imbalances, and taking refuge in abstraction and ambiguity rather than facing up to the challenges of the real world.

This matters because we are suffering from a serious deficit of political and social imagination. The oddity of the early decades of the twenty-first century is that it is easy now to imagine technological futures and easier still to imagine ecological disaster, not far in the future. But most people struggle to imagine or describe how our society, our democracy, our welfare, or our healthcare could evolve for the better over a generation or two. Our capacity to imagine has been stunted. Instead, pessimism and fatalism have become the default.

Art should be able to help. It can assist us in sensing what lies ahead. It can give us premonitions of possible futures, perhaps reflecting a collective unconscious in ways that conscious thought finds harder. It can help us sense the radical possibilities, both good and bad, that may lie ahead. It can point to a potential future of more advanced consciousness and more advanced collective intelligence.

It can show us our ambiguous power in the age of the Anthropocene and a possible post-human future, as we appreciate, with humility, our smallness in the vastness of the universe, and the contingency of our position amidst a multiplicity of life as well as novel intelligences.

But how? This Element investigates the different roles that the arts can play: the good and the bad, the beautiful and the ugly. It shows how artists are bearing witness to wrongs – from climate disaster and racism to human rights abuses – and how they can campaign, disrupt, and challenge. It describes methods, examples, and complexities, whether in visual art or literature, architecture, or film. And it reinforces the vital role the arts can play in cultivating a broader, wiser perspective on the world, as an antidote to narrow, linear, siloed thinking, and the polarisation that stems from lack of mutual understanding.

But it also argues that when the arts try too hard to prescribe or describe, when they are didactic, or when they seek too intently to serve a social or political goal, they become banal. It suggests a parallel with therapy. Many schools of therapy warn against the therapist being too explicit in their diagnosis: better to ask questions, open up new spaces for thought and feeling; better to nudge and suggest so that the patient can co-create their own answers.

In a similar way, the relationship of art to change is often strongest when it is most distant and artists are at their best when they are 'prophets at a tangent'; when they hint at what cannot yet be thought and said rather than trying to spell it out too literally.

The Element calls on artists to explore these tangents – the oblique angles – not to attempt to be social theorists or visionaries, but to experiment with images, words, and sounds, with dissonance as well as consonance, discord as well as harmony, to help us imagine other ways of being as well as doing. It encourages artists to immerse themselves in the frontiers of science and technology and of values and ways of living, to sense the possible directions of our future evolution, and then feed back an artistic imaginary that can, in turn, help others in their lives and work.

Art *can* be redemptive. But it redeems best when it redeems at a tangent, not head on.

Anticipating New Truth

For two hundred years we have been told that the arts blaze a trail for new ways of organising society. The poet Percy Bysshe Shelley claimed that 'poets are the unacknowledged legislators of the world'. Friedrich Schiller promised that art anticipates new truth 'preparing the shape of things to come'. More recently, Joseph Beuys (Figure 1), wrote that 'only art is capable of dismantling the

Figure 1 Joseph Beuys with bicycle. Archiv der Evangelischen Kirche im Rheinland from Düsseldorf/Boppard, Deutschland

repressive effects of a senile social system that continues to totter along the death-line'.

Such words are energising and inspiring, particularly at times, like now, that feel like they are moments of profound transition – away from an era when so much power and so many decisions were monopolised by white, rich, educated men and away from the high-waste, high-consumption economy which so defined the world in the last century.

All of these involve changes in how we see as well as how we act, and the arts have indeed repeatedly transformed perspectives. The Renaissance opened them up literally. Nineteenth-century art burst apart orthodox representations and transformed understandings of nature, often in opposition to rampant industrialisation.

These frontiers of perception change who we are and they cut across the boundaries of art, science, and thought. Da Vinci transformed how people saw their own anatomy. Turner's painting 'The Snowstorm' re-pictured the world through the lens of Faraday's new science of magnetism and electricity (showing the pattern achieved by holding a magnet beneath a sheet of paper covered with iron filings).

Today the arts are transforming how we observe the world around us, from the microscopic to the cosmic, showing patterns of emergence, combination, and evolution, or giving insights into the inner life of the mind: always challenging the dull orthodoxy of the normal. String theory in physics may be easier to imagine through the lens of music; quantum entanglement through poetry; the life of a cell through film.

The fact that we can now see what it looks like to be a protein, ambling or stumbling deep inside our body, that we can see, feel, or hear processes of decomposition, or what an event horizon looks like in space, transforms of our view of ourselves. Ubiquitous digital technologies break down the barriers between things and representations, and make everything amenable to deconstruction and reconstruction, programming and deprogramming, immersion as well as viewing or listening.

Some of these can be understood as hints of a shift in consciousness to something more collective, more open, more willing to accept many perspectives and experiences, valuing co-creation over passive consumption. Despite the power of competing twenty-first-century imaginaries, from the techno-nationalist authoritarianism of contemporary China to a revival of the Islamic Caliphate, I am convinced that it is meaningful to talk of an evolution of consciousness in the past and future, towards a bigger, more inclusive sense of us and our place in the universe, even if, by definition, it is impossible for any era to know with any certainty what the future evolution of consciousness will look like. The arts are, and should be, on the frontiers of these shifts. They help us in what Lola Olufemi calls a 'a firm embrace of the unknowable'.[1]

And yet. All over-confident claims that there are clear patterns linking changes in art to changes in other fields fall apart on closer inspection.[2] There certainly are analogies and parallels – and it would be surprising if there weren't. We live in at least partly integrated cultures – scientists visit art galleries, artists pick up on advances in science, novelists try to capture a zeitgeist in ways that make it coherent.

But in relation to social change, what's surprising is how little direct congruence there is between imaginative art and social imagination, not how much. Art can warn, denounce, and mock, prodding, scratching,[3] unsettling, opening up, and liberating. But the arts have done surprisingly little to influence how the world thinks about its social, economic, or political future.

This is true even of the most representational art forms. In the 1960s, a clutch of utopian novels – like Ursula LeGuin's *The Dispossessed* or Marge Piercy's *Woman on the Edge of Time* – portrayed a future beyond patriarchy and capitalism in ways that were inspiring as well as subtle.

More recent writings, like the cyberpunk novels of William Gibson, accurately predicted some of the textures of life in ever more digital environments, and many impressive works have explored both positive and negative ecological futures. But the last half century has brought no popular utopias, and no recent novels, films, works of visual art, or music can plausibly claim to have changed the world (later on, I discuss some of the partial exceptions – such as the work of Kim Stanley Robinson and Nicola Griffiths font seems bigger – and I look at the role of utopias in more detail, their uses and limitations).

So why might it be so hard for the arts, even the more representational arts like film and literature, to imagine, in a social sense? And how might a different kind of art help to amplify our shared dreams of a better society?

The rest of this Element suggests answers.

Section 1 shows why the arts are bound to struggle in contributing to social design and imagination: why the invisible patterns of social relationships are so hard to represent and how the political economy of art pulls it away from social engagement.

Section 2 looks at specific reasons why this is difficult now – in an era when the artist has become less godlike, when ideas can be so easily spread, manipulated, and combined.

Section 3 then describes the many roles the arts can and could play to help us prepare for and shape the transitions we need. It looks at perception, slow art, co-creation, rebellion and challenge, and hacking.

In Section 4, I look at how the different forms of art can respond: the role of political campaigns, literature, television and film, and architecture, and how the arts can explore the frontiers of technology.

Section 5 starts tying threads together, looking at the positive potential of an evolution of human collective consciousness, how this connects to changing values, and how tools for creativity could become more ubiquitous and more embedded in society.

Section 6 suggests a way of thinking about many of these dynamics in a dialectical rather than a linear way, with the arts, like social thought, both going with and against the grain of changes in technology and the economy.

Finally, in Section 7, I conclude by looking at how the arts can make us bigger, escaping from our constraints, and also more humble, at a time when the human-centric obsessions of recent centuries look ever less appropriate to the times we are in.

1 The Inherent Limitations of Art as a Tool for Social Imagination

During the course of this Element, I examine the unique role that the arts can play in helping us to think, see, and imagine differently. But here, I start with the negatives and look at why it might be *inherently* hard for the arts to imagine or describe the possible social arrangements of the near or far future.

Impossible Prediction

The most basic reason is simple and shared with every form of creative activity. The future cannot be known. Societies are vastly more complex than our brains. No one has done well in prediction. Many have described immanent processes or extrapolated from current trends. Some have predicted by mistake or made so many forecasts that some were bound to be right.

The designers of the future can do fairly well over a twenty-year time horizon spotting what is possible already (for example, how the climate might change, populations will age, or technologies spread). But they do much less well over longer time horizons, so there is no reason we should expect the arts to do much better. After all, which works of art in 1950 accurately proposed or predicted the world of the 2020s? Yes, some warned of ecological rupture; others advocated transformed gender relations or the blight of managerialism and technocracy. Before the First World War there were many intimations of impending disaster. But these ideas had been in the ether for a very long time already, and no artworks can be read in retrospect as an accurate prophecy, premonition, or prediction and it is probably foolish to expect that they could.

Invisible and Visible

The second reason for this gap is also simple. Imagination is by its nature visual, and this is the origin of the word. But social arrangements are invisible or at least their most important characteristics are. Power, relationships, and feelings of safety or agency cannot be easily seen, even if the places where they happen can be pictured and abstract diagrams can try to portray what's social.

The result is that artists struggle to visualise or, if they do so, risk descending to cliché, banality, or propaganda. The same is true of music. Both can be powerful as commentary or critique. They can embody a social view – like the thousands of people who lay on the ground of cities for Black Lives Matter or Extinction Rebellion, brilliantly embodying a shared view of what had gone badly wrong. But they are unable to propose. You cannot dance, paint, or sing a possible future constitution and probably shouldn't try.

Bearing Witness

This helps to explain a striking pattern: the arts are much better at warning or bearing witness than they are at prescribing. Olafur Eliasson's blocks of ice melting in city squares (see Figure 2) vividly make people think about climate change as a reality not an abstraction.

A similar effect is achieved by Andri Snær Magnason's plaque to commemorate a lost glacier in Iceland[4] or the World Meteorological Organization's short videos presenting fictional weather reports from different countries in the year 2050: *WMO Weather Reports 2050*.

Natasha Marin's exhibition in Seattle on Black Imagination is another good example, combining fragments, stories, experiences, and poetry of suffering and survival, to bring to life a very different perspective to that of the arts mainstream.

There is a long history of artworks that bore witness in this way, testifying to realities that were otherwise suppressed. Picasso's *Guernica* is one of the most famous, highlighting to the world the horrors of the destruction of the Basque town in an act that prefigured the mass bombing of civilians that characterised the World War that started only a few years later.

Figure 2 *Ice Watch* by Olafur Eliasson and Minik Rosing
Source: Jorge Láscar from Melbourne, Australia, CC BY 2.0, via Wikimedia Commons

Jacob Lawrence's *Great Migration* series, painted in the early 1940s, showed the lives of former slaves who were desperate to escape the southern United States and head for the cities of the north in search of freedom and a better life.

In the 1980s, Act-Up's slogan 'Silence=Death', plastered on many walls, helped to force action on AIDs. Art served here as an alarm, a shouting, shrieking call to take seriously a horror that was happening but being ignored.

A more recent and different example is JR, with his extraordinary, huge works that he calls 'Pervasive Art', spread across Brazilian favelas, cities in Palestine and Israel, or Parisian housing estates. These (initially) illegal works of flyposting were meant to break down the barriers between spectators and participants as old and young were mobilised to play their part in the act of creation and their images were made into vast displays, reclaiming the city and turning the street into an art gallery.

Ai Wei Wei is perhaps the most striking contemporary example of an artist bearing witness, using his blog, documentary, video, sculpture, and other art works, to expose human rights abuses and corruption, notably after the 2008 Sichuan earthquake. The crass reactions of the authorities – from the demolition of his studio to his trial on tax charges – become part of the performance, as the state confirms its inability to accept inconvenient truths.

Such highly political bearing of witness has a long history, through to recent times when the music of Thomas Mapfumo bore witness to the liberation struggle in Zimbabwe, serving to motivate and reinforce the conviction of the population fighting to overthrow white rule.

Bearing witness can take many forms, from fiction to the fantastic. Shostakovich's Seventh Symphony was thought to bear witness to the siege of Leningrad (even though he conceived it before the war), acknowledging an extraordinary story of human suffering. The recent documentary *Babyn Yar* by Sergei Loznitsa is a contemporary example. With no voice-overs or dramatic music, but with a brilliant reconstruction of images and sounds, it chronicles the 1941 massacre of hundreds of thousands of Jews near Kyiv under the Nazis, but also bears witness to the uncomfortable fact that many in the region at first welcomed the invaders. The film's physical cousin in Kyiv, constructed by Ilya Khrzhanovsky on the site of the massacre, is set, subject to the vicissitudes of war, to be almost a new art form in its own right, melding history, religion (a church, a mosque, and a synagogue), interactive exhibits and virtual reality (VR), and perhaps more (at one point the idea of visitors doing role plays was floated, which prompted a wave of public revulsion).

Hollywood films like *Wall-E* and *Avatar* offer a simpler kind of bearing witness, bringing a critical ecological consciousness into the mainstream, as have documentaries like James Cameron's *Years of Living Dangerously* or David Attenborough's *A Life on our Planet*.

Ben Grosser is a good example of bearing witness for a digital age. His videos have lambasted the power of Facebook, with one pulling together every public example of Mark Zuckerberg talking about 'more' and 'bigger' into a compelling, horrific montage. He has created new apps – demetricators – to help people remove the metrics from their use of the big platforms, Facebook, Twitter, TikTok; the addictive 'likes' that exploit our dopamine systems and hook us with the appearance of social approval. He has also created a tool designed to disrupt government surveillance, adding random words to emails that are likely to set off alarm bells in the National Security Agency (bomb, suicide, Allah …). Interestingly, he also points out that if the great artists of the past had been so intently obsessed with immediate approval they might have shied away from their greatest art. Here we see the contemporary artist as provocateur and disrupter, embarrassing power and connecting to a very long traditions of jesters, jokers, and mockers.

At their best, these many ways of bearing witness to things going awry in our society are moving and not just clever, opening up ways of seeing into the gut and heart as well as the head: 'below the neck' awareness that is such a vital complement to awareness above the neck.

They are a vital part of how we understand others – strangers with whom we may appear to have little in common. The immersive quality of novels, poetry, paintings, and films have all made it possible to enter other peoples' minds, and escape the confines of our own worlds and circles, opening up richer empathy and understanding.

But, to the extent that such works of bearing witness have a broader social message, it's usually quite simple. They are a spark. Someone else has to then do the hard work of translating that spark into ideas or politics.

A similar impulse of warning and educating lies behind the many artworks made of discarded rubber or other kinds of waste. For them, the medium is the message, criticising the wastefulness of consumer capitalism and prompting a different way of seeing and a different aesthetic.[5] But they too are a stimulus rather than a deep reflection, let alone an account or a proposal. They need something additional, beyond their own creations, to dig deep.[6]

2 The Retreat from Prophecy: From Gods to Commentators, Direct to Indirect, Obvious to Opaque

If these are some of the reasons why it's hard for the arts to imagine in social terms, even as the arts are uniquely able to bear witness to wrongs and threats, there are also some very specific factors in play now. The nineteenth and twentieth centuries elevated the (typically male) artist into something close to being a god: Beethoven, Picasso, Tolstoy, even film directors like Kubrick or Tarkovsky, are obvious examples. No one quite plays such a role today.[7] Social media have democratised artistic production. Millions can make films, music, or texts, and the boundary between professionals and amateurs is even harder to police than it was in the past. Digital technologies have also brought an explosive capacity to copy, recombine, and distort, which makes the very idea of an individual style, or individual ownership, look like an anachronism.

The shift is far from complete. As David Hopkins points out in his history of late twentieth-century art, despite calls for the death of the author, 'the prestige of individual artists has continued to be paramount',[8] helped by the star systems of contemporary culture which turn a tiny number of creators into truly global icons. But despite their visibility, and 'brand value', their authority is not what it was.

Meanwhile deeper shifts in values have challenged the claims of any elite groups. For twentieth-century Western liberal democracies, the freedom of the (again, usually male) artist was treated as almost sacred. Their right to offend, disrupt, and challenge was defended as the mark of an advanced civilisation. The more offensive artists were, the more admired they were for their courage.

Yet the generations growing up in the twenty-first century see these rights as less absolute. They are more likely to believe that artists should be accountable for their actions and beliefs, particularly on issues of race, gender, and sexuality, fuelling sharp intergenerational tensions.

The emerging global hive mind that's being experimented with by many artists sometimes seems to offer a premonition of a future society based on collective intelligence and greater mutual accountability. This could be taken as confirmation of Marshall McLuhan's suggestion that art can 'anticipate future social and technological developments', providing what he called 'indispensable perceptual training'.[9] But it also leaves the individual artist with a diminished role – less like an Old Testament prophet pointing the way to the promised land, and more like a commentator, nudging, subverting, and suggesting.

The Changing Role of the Artist

As the role of the artist has changed, so has the content. There was a time when art could be very straightforward and direct – in praise of a saint or ruler, or portraying a familiar event like the crucifixion, for example. But the nearer to the present we come, the more artists shy away from transparency, obviousness, and meaning. That was, in part, a movement from nature to abstraction: from a metaphysical problem of understanding form and space in the natural world to the purely aesthetic problem of grasping and using pure form and space in painting, sculpture, music, and architecture.

Artists are, in part, responding to their audience. Today we don't like being 'told what to think', 'preached at', or 'lectured to' (even though we are, all the time), because this implies a passivity, a stupidity, an asymmetry between the preacher and the preached to. So we prefer this to be dressed up as shared discovery, 'showing not telling', signalling indirectly rather than directly.

This makes it hard for art to be revolutionary in the traditional sense of directly serving a cause or portraying the promised land, in the way that revolutions once co-opted art. Eisenstein's films turned the Russian revolution into an epic drama with the proletariat as hero. Dovzhenko's *The Earth* (see Figure 3) is a masterpiece and also an extraordinary spiritual paean to collectivisation in Ukraine in 1930 (which at the time was causing the deaths of millions). The Mexican murals of Diego Rivera, Orozco, and Siqueiros in a similar spirit turned the people into heroes of their own drama,[10] and there are many examples of art providing a backdrop and a soundtrack for political change, whether for Fidel Castro in Cuba or for the ANC in South Africa.

But now artists quickly become uncomfortable if they are expected to be servants of politics. They prefer to be opaque, not obvious. Gerhard Richter summed up the late twentieth-century ethic well: 'pictures which are interpretable, and which contain a meaning, are bad pictures'. Good pictures, by contrast, 'take away our certainty … show us the thing in all the manifold

Figure 3 Still from the film *The Earth* by Alexander Dovzhenko.
Source: Alexander Dovzhenko, Public domain, via Wikimedia Commons

significance and infinite variety that preclude the emergence of any single meaning and view'.[11] The postmodern ethos, which has been so influential in the arts, encourages a playful, ironic scepticism of any absolutes or certainty, let alone any sense that history might have a meaning or direction. It echoes the position of modernists a century ago, who constantly struggled against leftists: the former emphasising ambiguity and the personal against the latter who wanted to subordinate art to political struggle.

Most of the highly regarded artists of our times like to shape-shift for just this reason, avoiding being too tied to any style or ethos. In their lives and their art, they opt for versions of the deliberate randomisation of early twentieth-century serial music which can occasionally throw up interesting new patterns but also risk draining meaning and coherence out of works: 'freedom with nothing left to push against except the empty air' is Jacques Barzun's phrase on the excesses of twentieth-century art.

This shift is encouraged by the ineptness of some attempts to be more overtly political. At the Venice Biennale in 2019, Christoph Buchel put on show a ship in which 1,000 migrants had died in the Mediterranean. He wanted to prompt a discussion, and it did indeed remind people of the appalling tragedies happening every day a few miles from Europe's southern borders. But the commentary was critical of artists appropriating others' suffering for their own glory and vanity and adding nothing to insight.

A more effective approach, perhaps, was the Crossroads Foundation creation of 'Refugee Run: A Day in the Life of a Refugee' in which participants 'face simulated attacks, mine fields … hunger, illness, lack of education, corruption and uncertain shelter or safety. Participants may also be marched under guard, subjected to ambush and, ultimately, offered a chance of re-settlement where they must re-build their lives.' This may not be everyone's definition of art, but it certainly promotes a new way of seeing and understanding.

Parallel challenges face any artists seeking to follow one of their other traditional roles, making the familiar seem other. 'Estrangement' is vital for opening up space for social imagination; seeing the oddity, or absurdity, of governments and leaders, and showing how artificial our apparently natural social arrangements are, makes it easier to imagine radical alternatives. Yet many of the social movements of our times are precisely set up to combat the 'othering' done to them by mainstream power – whether in relation to gender, race, sexuality, empire, or disability. The last thing a marginal group needs is to be made even more other and strange. So, although one good artistic response is to flip things around and play with the strangeness of the established order, any playing with strangeness has also become perilous territory.

All of these problems of the relationship between art and politics are perhaps reinforced by the oddness of twentieth-century history. In the nineteenth century, it was just plausible that greater engagement with the arts would tend to mean a more enlightened and progressive view of the world. But the political leader of the twentieth century who was most engaged with the arts was probably Adolf Hitler, a former artist who hoped to become an artist again in retirement, who intervened in the detail of plays and operas, hosted artists of all kinds, and who cast his political project as just as much about aesthetics as institutions. Never again would it be possible to believe that art is by its nature redemptive.[12]

Art against Rules and Algorithms

Another contemporary reason for the uncomfortable relationship between art and social imagination is the parallel tension between the ideals of art and the realities of organisation, and how social problems get fixed in the real world.

Much of what we count as progress has involved the world becoming more structured and organised. Better organisation is why life expectancy is so much higher and child mortality so much lower than in the past. It's why billions of people are so much more prosperous and so much less vulnerable to violence than their grandparents. By most measures – life expectancy, health, prosperity, security from the risk of violent death – the world has never had it so good and today's generations are extraordinarily lucky, even if our culture often tells an opposite story, and notwithstanding the huge costs that accompanied the progress and the huge threats that lie ahead.

Although many older traditions loved order, this is a difficult story for contemporary art to accept. It is easier for art to stand against the iron cages of rationality, denouncing the more extreme examples of the juggernauts of progress, as the early nineteenth-century romantics denounced industrialisation and the railways, and as later generations denounced Stalin's collectivisation, Mao's Great Leap Forward, the roads of New York's Robert Moses, Le Corbusier's cities, and all the many examples of the folly of design and the hubris of progress that crushed intimacy, community, and family.

The Marvel heroes are a classic example today, with a series of simple tropes that precisely mirror the romantic ideal: action over thought, the individual over institutions, beauty over ugliness, heroic deeds the result of inherent capabilities rather than education or hard work.

Yet the progress that we take for granted was the product of social movements that fuelled new bureaucracies, institutions, measurements, laws, and plans. The heat of the movements mutated into the cool of systems and structures. Progress on equality, child mortality, or pollution would have been impossible without large-scale systems that were often the antithesis of individual creativity. Looking to the future, if the world is to avert the horrors of climate catastrophe, it will come, in part, because of the introduction of new rules, taxes, and constraints that come about as a result of the campaigns, marches, strikes, and petitions.

A similar tension surrounds algorithms and data. These both liberate and constrain us at the same time. It's data that allows us to analyse carbon emissions or air quality, or new patterns of inequality, and algorithms can be used to spot biases and discrimination (though they can, of course, also embed past biases, too).

Ever since the Industrial Revolution, artists have tended to emphasise the restrictions and limitations that this progress brings rather than the benefits (and even long before the Industrial Revolution, Chinese landscape art was intended to provide its civil servants with an escape from bureaucratic mundanity, a counterpoint to the human order they were meant to impose).

For the romantics who set much of the tone for the modern artistic sensibility, structure was the enemy. They favoured free love over marriage; the spontaneous life over the tyranny of factory or office, nature over civilisation, the nomad over the farmer. Theirs was a world of energy and flux. They were uncomfortable with any moves to turn that energy into structure, the transition of hot to cool that is essential to all social change and progress.[13]

Today, too, many artists warn of the new iron cages being brought by ubiquitous algorithms. This is very apparent in the extraordinary upsurge of art works both using, and playing with, the potential of Artificial Intelligence (AI). Look, for example, at the work of the Nabi Art Center under Soh Yeong Roh in South Korea exploring 'neotopias' of all kinds and how data may reinvent or dismantle our humanity, or exploring the role of social robots – some shaped like animal pets – as emotionally subtle friends for the elderly or teenagers in an increasingly lonely world (in a society that has also led with new innovations like daytime discos for the elderly). LuYang's brilliant *Delusional Mandala* (see Figure 4) investigates the brain, imagination, and AI, connecting neuroscience and religious experience to our new-found powers to create strange avatars.

The capacity of AI to generate increasingly plausible works of visual art and music is, of course, a direct threat to artists, and perhaps encourages a hostile or at least sceptical response in works like Hito Steyerl's projects exploring surveillance and robotics (like HellYeahWeFuckDie); Trevor Paglen playing with mass surveillance and AI; or Sun Yuan and Peng Yu's 'Can't Help Myself', on out-of-control robots.

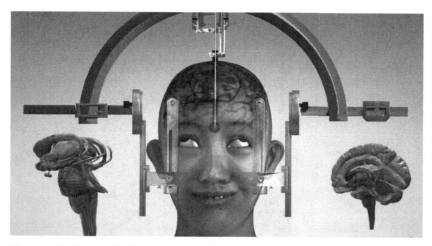

Figure 4 Still from LuYang's *Delusional Mandala*, © Lu Yang, www.artsy.net/artwork/lu-yang-luyang-delusional-mandala-1, with thanks to the artist

Others are more ambiguous. Ian Cheng's *Emissaries* series imagined a post-apocalyptic world of AI fauna, while Sarah Newman's work, such as the *Moral Labyrinth*, explores in a physical space how robots might mirror our moral choices, giving a flavour of a future where algorithms guide our behaviours. Andreas Refsgaard's work is playful in a similar vein, like the algorithm assessing whether people are trustworthy enough to be allowed to ask questions. Shu Lea Cheang's work *3x3x6* (see Figure 5) references the standards for modern prisons with 3×3-square-meter cells monitored continuously by six cameras, using this to open up questions about surveillance and sousveillance, and the use of facial recognition technologies to judge sexuality (including in parts of the world where it's illegal to be gay).

Each of these brings to the surface the opaque new systems of power and decision that surround us, the hugely complex problems of ethical judgement that come with powerful AI, and the role of error and imperfection in evolution and human progress. Each is preparing us for a future – and for many a present – where our lives constantly interact with machine intelligence.

There is a parallel story of artists using AI as a tool – with GPT3 writing fiction, Google Tiltbrush and Daydream in VR, or the growing use of AI by musicians and composers – and many wonderful examples of emerging art forms (like Refik Anadol's *Quantum Memories* at the National Gallery of Victoria in Melbourne, shown in Figure 6). But most engagement has been cautiously critical, and most pictures of the future involving artists are negative, encouraging fear rather than hope.

Figure 5 Still from *3x3x6* by Shu Lea Cheang, with thanks to the artist

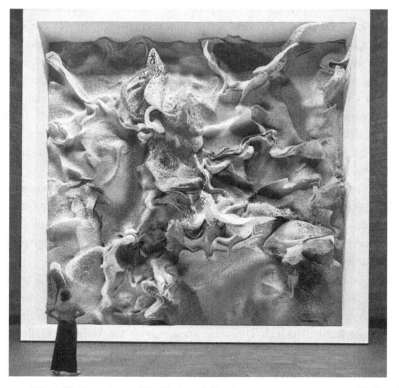

Figure 6 Installation view of Refik Anadol's *Quantum Memories*, on display in NGV Triennial 2020. Photograph: Refik Anadol

In the 1960s, Gilles Deleuze suggested that societies were moving from discipline to control, and from moulding to modulation, and these new types of art can perhaps be understood as helping us to see how we are being modulated, and how we might resist.[14] But again, this is art as champion of freedom against restraint, and art as perception and warning rather than as design, and in all of these examples the artists are more comfortable in the role of jeremiad – warning of lost humanity, warmth, and wisdom – or playfully pulling apart the strange dynamics of networked relationships, rather than offering even a fuzzy route to a better future.[15]

The Political Economy of Art in Capitalism and the Risks of Easy Co-option

Another reason why this is so difficult is the political economy of art, or, to put it more starkly, the relationship of art to capitalism. Many artists see themselves as enemies of capitalism: of a system that knows the price of everything and the value of nothing. But it's not easy to insulate yourself from its logic.

A century ago, Walter Benjamin, in his famous essay on 'Art in an Age of Mechanical Reproduction', discussed how art had lost its aura and authenticity as first photography, and then recorded sound and film, turned art works into commodities, abundant and no longer magical.[16] One response of the art world then was retreat – into the idea of art for art's sake, which Benjamin called the 'theology of art' – that would at least protect it from challenge. For many, that has remained a safe haven, and the great festivals of music, film, or art still project an almost religious spirit, believing themselves to be antidotes to the ugliness and corruption of the world around them. Indeed, the aura of authentic, original art remains perhaps just as strong: if it were not, it would be impossible to explain the extraordinary prices that artworks now achieve, particularly contemporary ones.

But the rise of mechanical reproduction had two other big effects which weren't foreseen. One is that it often furthered the division between elites and the masses. As Pierre Bourdieu showed, culture quickly becomes a way of asserting distinction – a way for the knowledge workers to assert their superiority over not just the poor but also competing elites through the books they read or the films they love or the galleries they visit or their preference for handmade goods and artisanal food.[17] Of course, the distinction dynamic works in reverse too, as rejection of these same art works becomes a way for others to prove their authenticity, denouncing the same elites for their arrogance and for being out of touch. The result is that it has become harder than ever to create art that is both pioneering as art and also inclusive (and most creative industries remain as socially skewed in their employment patterns and their audience patterns as ever).

The division between high and low art has brought with it another odd social dynamic too, with public subsidy (which in theory was more socialist) tending to be monopolised by elite and traditional art forms (opera, theatre, galleries) while the working classes consumed mainly popular culture, often from the United States (Hollywood to Motown to rap).[18] Artists could insulate themselves from capitalism if they could find a generous source of state patronage, but usually that meant being locked into an elite audience.

Meanwhile, the upper echelons of the visual arts are utterly interwoven with the lives and economy of the super-rich, having opted to ally much more with high fashion than low politics. This isn't entirely new. Throughout history, artists have depended on the patronage of the wealthy. Matisse may have had his tongue in his cheek when he said that his paintings should serve as an 'armchair for the tired businessman' but he was also being honest.

The result is an odd mix of rhetorical piety and practical pluto-philia, even more evident in architecture, which depends so much on commissions from the top 0.001 per cent. Read the blurbs for biennales of all kinds (with the vague nods to ecology, community, and the commons) and these contradictions become painfully obvious. Vague piety combines with sycophancy to the very rich, which dissolves only in extreme cases when the media bring the most uncomfortable truths to the surface – as happened when the arts world had to separate from the Sacklers, spurning their generous philanthropy, as the extent of their role in America's opiate epidemic became unavoidable.

For those who have avoided dependence on the state or the very rich, the options are no more straightforward. Banksy is a classic example, a brilliantly playful artist who made fun of the absurdity of the art market by shredding one of his works – *Love is in the Bin* – in an auction house, just after selling it for nearly £1 m, an act that was clever and funny, though taking on a pretty easy target. There are now plenty of exciting, irreverent, disruptive artists all over the world keeping alive some of the spirit of Dada, Situationism, and the other twentieth-century movements that enjoyed mocking and undermining the pomposity of the arts establishment.[19]

Some are experimenting with new forms of ownership – using blockchain and NFT (non-fungible tokens) to allow for ownership of unique digital artworks – with new approaches to exhibition such as the B20 museum.[20]

But it's far from clear whether the disrupting is really disrupting anything very much. The NFT mania may be little more than a new bubble for the rich to speculate with. You can now buy hundreds of Banksy works online (masterworks.io encourages customers to 'skip our waitlist to invest in paintings by artists like Banksy and Basquiat with 10–25% historical appreciation'). For decades many products have mocked consumer capitalism, such as a McDonald's image of a burger turned into the slogan 'eat the rich'. But, like Che Guevara t-shirts, they inadvertently prove just how easily capitalism can absorb its critics.

Music is particularly prone to this: good at making people feel rebellious and transgressive, but not so good at actually drawing blood. As Mark Fisher explained in his book *Capitalist Realism: Is There No Alternative?*: 'even success mean[s] failure'.[21] Musicians want audiences, but the more popular they are the more they become enmeshed in the commercial system.[22] The arts help people to disrupt their own identities, but in safe ways – white teenagers loving rap, rich buyers spending a fortune on a Bastiat or Banksy.

Of course, the arts have always been closely woven into the economic power structures of their times. Andy Warhol was a commercial artist and creator of window displays for New York stores, as was Jasper Johns, and Pop Art was a perfect fusion of mass consumer capitalism and high art. It is perhaps unfair to expect them to be subversive in any meaningful way: as Audrey Lorde famously put it, 'the master's tools will never dismantle the master's house .... They may allow us temporarily to beat him at his own game, but they will never enable us to bring about genuine change.'[23]

The logical conclusion of these syntheses of capitalism and advanced art was that the individual life became the site of making art through consumption and self-reflection, a trend accelerated by social media and Instagram, posing, styling, seeking affirmation from the crowd, connecting us back to an ancient time when the body was the canvas, with tattoos and jewellery, but also providing an escape from any possibility of collective action.

This is the trend developed by Cindy Sherman and extended by figures like Marina Abramovich, another brilliant artist, who creates an intimate engagement with audiences in a present that makes no claim to either a past or a future; a dramatically slowed down present where you, and the artist, can be anything, and where you stand on the edge of discomfort but where your identity or meaning as part of anything bigger has been erased.

Now as we enter an era when AI can not only reproduce art, but also reproduce styles, adapt, enhance, and amplify, even more complex patterns are likely: a proliferation of artworks whose provenance is hard to guess; a further democratisation of cultural production, as anyone can become at least a plausible painter, composer, or film director; and perhaps an even greater allure for the direct, the human, the tangible, and the authentic in response.

Walter Benjamin quoted Pirandello on the strangeness that overcomes the actor in front of a camera. Now we all experience an even greater strangeness as our image, our voice, and everything about us can be mutated on screens in front of us or in a virtual reality as we, and our mutating representations, become a loop in which action and observation are inseparable, and in which we are perhaps irredeemably liberated from the assumption that there is an objective and coherent 'I'.

Perhaps ahead of us lies a world where the aura that Benjamin thought had gone returns, but this time ushered in by technology. After all, artificial intelligence is already often beyond our comprehension and in the near future will become even more opaque, baffling, and magical, capable of creating wonders and ecstasies, presided over by avatars, as our sense of the human slowly diminishes.

Imagination in the Economy and Society: Being Big in Life

The odd disengagement from both individual identity and from collective social change we have described becomes even clearer if we look at how the broader capitalist economy has appropriated ideals that were once exclusive to the arts. The romantics of the eighteenth and early nineteenth centuries believed that imagination was nothing less than a life force, indeed that cultivating and expanding the imagination made us more human.[24] They believed that we should never be content merely with the rhythms of everyday life. Instead, they tried to spark ambition and had a mission to make this contagious – to spread, inspire, and infect others with a sense of historic possibility, helping others to reflect on their place not just in the world of family, friends, and work but also to look out from the mountain top with the full sweep of history at their feet. To be heroes, not just for one day but for all time.

This leap of faith and confidence was, and always is, irrational. There can never be enough justification for the leaps involved, and most fail. But the ideal of self-transcendence has remained powerful, as has its twin idea of self-subversion, the idea that you should actively challenge and so transform yourself.

This ideal spread in philosophy and literature and was particularly powerful amongst the poets. It promised a religious passion – acknowledging that the infinite could be found within the finite, the spark of spirit inside each individual. It suggested that we are only fully human in the moments when we shape and change our world – so preferring the crowd marching in the streets to the slog of bureaucratic structures, the Dionysian festival to the serried ranks of the concert hall. It saw freedom in those moments when we escape structure before it comes back and crushes the spirit.

For most of the last two centuries, imagination stood in opposition to government, order, and stultifying conformity. It also seemed to stand in opposition to the economy with its factories, repetition, destruction of nature, billowing smoke, and the noise of the machinery and the trains.

But, in the later years of the twentieth century, a strange shift has left this pattern drastically changed. The main reason is that the economy has mutated to become an agent of a very similar idea of imagination. Novelty has come to be seen as the motor of growth: R&D, innovation, and new ideas summoned up from anywhere – whether costly research laboratories or the flash of inspiration in the mind of the entrepreneur and innovator – now fuel GDP. The creative industries and a broader creative economy have come to be seen as emblematic not exceptions, constantly seeking to remake, recombine, and reimagine music, film, the arts, and making wealth out of thin air. Around it have grown new systems for generating capital, public subsidy, and training, new measurements, and new ways of harnessing imagination for products. Where, in a previous era, the machine and the human were presented as alternatives, in this world they are complements, the skill of the imaginative musician or film director amplified by a battery of techniques.

The creative imagination of the twenty-first century, therefore, encourages a very different mentality to the problem-solving of the engineer or the bureaucrat, with designers jumping straight to solutions and immersing themselves in previously unimagined problems. To help them, business has supported factories of imagination – film studios employing thousands on SFX; design and advertising studios manipulating images and ideas; big teams producing complex online games with hundreds of millions of players. All are commodities in one sense but quite unlike other commodities. And so, a dynamic economy has grown up feeding some kinds of imagination, and the romantic ideal lives on but in attenuated form in the life of creative workers, which tends to be less predictable than others – organised around projects, uncertain timescales and results.

The odd thing, however, is that although this economy is well designed for imagining new ways of achieving pleasure and products that encourage repeated use, as well as hardware of all kinds, it has done nothing to feed social imagination. What was institutionalised in the realms of culture, and to a lesser extent, science, has in no way been institutionalised for society itself; indeed, social imagination may even have been squeezed out.

The rise of an economy of imagination has also had a subtler effect. The hope of the romantics had been to overthrow the machine-like, formulaic industrial culture – that turned people into modular cogs with no room to imagine or breathe – and offer, in its place, the imaginative connected mind, seeing the links of everything to everything else – cosmic, ecological, systemic, and able to constantly challenge and subvert itself and everything else in permanent revolution.

In pockets and places this ideal has grown roots – in milieux that encourage civic energy, and the cross-pollination of creative industries, social innovation, and technology. But many experienced a big gulf between the ethic and the reality. The ethic was of living a creative life, with hacking, experiment, and free spirits. The reality is more often that of highly organised, oligopolistic digital industries run in big hierarchical companies; or an art world that played at radical shock but no longer worried anyone as the prices hurtled upwards; or of radicalism turned into lifestyle; or of media that offered voyeuristic imagination with little power to stir the soul.

The utopian promise was still that machines would take over all the dull repeatable tasks and free everyone else for the promise of Marx:

> In communist society, where nobody has one exclusive sphere of activity but each can become accomplished in any branch he wishes, society regulates the general production and thus makes it possible for me to do one thing today and another tomorrow, to hunt in the morning, fish in the afternoon, rear cattle in the evening, criticise after dinner, just as I have a mind, without ever becoming hunter, fisherman, herdsman or critic.[25]

By doing the repeatable, machines would free us to do the unrepeatable.

But this has remained as much a fantasy for the vast majority as ever, as they are still either stuck within organisations or cast as a new precariat with even less real freedom. They are left ever further from Keats' 'negative capability', and also without the legal and institutional frameworks that might allow autonomous labour to match the scale and reach of capital.

The political effects have been worse still, since what has resulted from the rise of an economy based on intangibles is a new divide between a relatively mobile, educated, and relatively well-remunerated minority allowed to use their minds and even imaginations, and a majority who are more constrained, experiencing often declining rewards with automation, and who are as a result ever more resentful of the cognitive elites, and their cultural contempt or separation from manual work, or work rooted in place. Here, imagination hits politics, and the artistic spirit, far from representing emancipation for the poor and the weak comes to be a privilege of the affluent and powerful, symbolised perhaps in the demographics of the most avid users of art galleries and concert halls.

The Ambiguous Relationship between Ethics and Aesthetics

An even less comfortable aspect of the relationship of art to social imagination is the relationship of aesthetics to ethics, and the hope that art is in some ways by definition on the side of the angels and the good.

The poet John Keats thought that beauty and truth were intimately related. Sometimes they are. The beauties of mathematics can reflect profound truths about the nature of the universe. But, in other fields, their relationship is much fuzzier. Truths can be ugly or banal. Beauty can be misleading or a trap. Indeed, this is a dilemma for arts of all kinds. They can sit aside from ethics, or right and wrong, and art works are often most powerful if they include within themselves ambiguities and contradictions rather than seeking to resolve them (as Stanislavski advised his actors, if you're playing someone evil, seek out their kindness).

But the other risk of art of all kinds is that it bypasses our logic, our doubt, and our scepticism. It pulls us along. This is the attraction of patriotic songs and military brass bands. It is why propaganda films – like Leni Riefenstahl's *The Triumph of the Will* – can be admired as great art even if their message is abhorrent. Sometimes the pleasure of art even comes from this feeling of being manipulated, a phenomenon visible in all political and social movements.

Deranged imagination is as much a part of our history as creative social imagination. The Festival of the Supreme Being, which was organised on a massive scale in Paris in 1794, is a good example. The brilliant artist Jacques-Louis David was in charge, working for Robespierre who was the effective leader of the government. The idea was to celebrate a new secular religion for a newly liberated people. It was certainly imaginative. But it was also dark and destructive and coincided with the terror of mass guillotining that a few months later would end Robespierre's life.

Stalin's manipulation not just of folk music and socialist realist art is well known, as is his uncomfortable relationship with great artists like Shostakovich. Less well-known are examples like Eisenstein's famous unfinished, and largely lost, film *Bezhin Meadow*: technically impressive, rich in religious symbolism and often beautiful in its portrayal of the Russian landscape, its core is the celebration of a child who denounces his parents. Its message, in other words, is one that many find morally repugnant, in service to a regime at the height of its murderous powers.

It is perhaps a reminder that we should always be suspicious of anything overly simple – art which presents one side as good and others as evil, reinforcing a simple world view. This is particularly important in the world of ideas. The simple idea may be beautiful in its simplicity – as the ideas of communism, neoclassical economics, or Salafi Islam are – to the extent that they intoxicate clever believers in their aesthetics but then blind them to the parts not explained, not thought through.

The very best perfumes include some hint of decay. In the same way for social imagination, as for music and art, simplicity and purity need additions to make them fit for the world.

After all, history rarely moves in neat lines. Hegel called this the 'ruse of reason' or history, which regularly twists intentions and plans into results that are contrary to what was hoped for. Contemporary examples include how America's actions to wipe out terrorism in the Middle East had the opposite effect, or how Hitler's aim of destroying communism instead strengthened it. Many violent revolutions resemble a Möbius strip rather than a straight road, so that moving in one direction turns out to take people to a place opposite to the one they expect. All are good reasons to be suspicious of overly neat, simplifying ideas, and instead to listen intently to subtler, messier descriptions of reality.

3 Ethos, Art, and Social Imagination: Exploring the Tangents

If these are some of the limits to the role of the arts in social imagination, what can they do? And what can they do uniquely? Luckily there are many answers to these questions, though they are often very different from the romantic ideal of the artist as visionary prophet.

Cultivating New Perspective and Critical Consciousness

The first answer takes us back to where we started: the role of the arts in changing how we see, hear, or experience. These are changes of perspective in its widest sense, that help us see the lives and pain of others or the dynamics of our planet.

Schopenhauer put this well when he wrote that 'the artist is not aware in abstract terms of the intention and purpose' of their work, and rather works 'unconsciously, "by feeling" in truth instinctively'.[26] This sensing is indirect, not fully digested or articulated, suggestive rather than prescriptive.

So, too, today artists help us hear things differently; to see the nano and the cosmic, or like some recent VR, such as Marshmallow's installation *We Live in an Ocean of Air* (Figure 7) to feel what it's like to be a tree; or to imagine ourselves in the shoes of someone experiencing the world in very different ways to us; or to think metaphorically, understanding social change as like a dance.[27]

If the artistic experience is compelling then, by analogy, we may be able to see our society or our economy in novel ways too, with our minds loosened up from the default of seeing social arrangements as more fixed than they actually are.

Figure 7 Marshmallow Laser Feast, Marshmallow installation, *We Live in an Ocean of Air*, Saatchi Gallery: www.thegalleryguide.co.uk/exhibitions/marsh mallow-laser-feast-we-live-ocean-air

By engaging with art in these ways we perhaps come closer to 'wide-awakeness' – an ideal of many Buddhist and Zen traditions[28] or to a more political variant of the kind proposed by Paolo Freire who spoke of 'conscientization' or critical consciousness[29]: understanding the world through new perspectives prompted by art, and then by reflection and action.

After all, most of us most of the time suppress awareness of a myriad of things – the feelings of others, the historical roots of present conditions, guilts and blames, injustices, not to mention the perspectives of physical objects (the 'non-duality' that Buddhism promotes). We do so in part because life is so much easier with less awareness. But art forms help us to see things afresh, as William Blake put it, cleansing the doors of perception.[30] They can also help us to reintegrate and synthesise, seeing things as wholes, perhaps returning us to the medieval world where the 'quadrivium', the essential curriculum of arithmetic, geometry, astronomy, and music, sat on top of the trivium (rhetoric, logic, and grammar) providing a coherent view of the world in which the later divisions between science and art made little sense.

Through this more holistic, and aware, perspective we can also see our own perceptions, becoming more conscious of our consciousness and aware of our awareness, in a loop that keeps reverberating afterwards, on the boundaries, the peripheries of knowledge and reason. In this way, the arts can open up metaphorical thought by a loosening process, and can play the role McLuhan suggested, of perceptual training ahead of social change.

The writer Jean Gebser provides a good starting point for putting this in a more systematic way. In the mid-twentieth century, his classic book, *The Ever-Present Origin*, made sweeping claims about how parallel shifts in perception affect everything from science to architecture, politics to everyday life.[31] Gebser was interested in how consciousness evolves, in jumps, to what he called a 'wakeful presence'. These jumps could be traced through history in a series of stages from the archaic (the most basic consciousness where humans didn't think of themselves as separate from the world) to the magical, where things are not representations but are the things themselves, understood outside time and space.

Next came a mythical consciousness that links these to rhythms of time, then came what he called a 'mental' stage – logical, rational, demythologised, and the foundation of science. Finally, he thought we were entering an integral stage in which time was reconceived, and the connectedness of past, present, and future was recognised, and the making present of things.

The crucial point is that Gebser thought that these shifts happen in all forms of thought: in art, science, religion, and politics as well as in daily life. Where biological evolution is thought of as progressive within the constraints of an environment, optimising animals and plants to the conditions of deserts, jungles, or tundra, these transformations were opposite in nature, opening up new possibilities and transforming environments as well as us.

Since Gebser wrote his magnum opus, many have taken up these ideas, notably Clare Graves and Ken Wilber. There is much to dispute in the details of their accounts. But some of the broad patterns fit quite well with the evidence from anthropology and prehistory and there clearly are some commonalities between thought in many domains.

Much of Gebser's thinking was prompted by art, perhaps not surprisingly since he was a friend of Picasso's. A central distinction in his work is between what he called 'perspectival' and 'unperspectival' art. Unperspectival art is the way a small child draws, before they learn to understand contexts and backgrounds (for Gebser this was the pattern of the archaic, magical, and mythical).

'Perspectival' is what you then learn – arranging elements in a clear way, with horizons and order (the essence of the 'mental' stage of consciousness). 'Aperspectival' art comes beyond that, as in Picasso's work, where multiple perspectives can coexist in what he called an 'integral consciousness'.

For Gebser, this pattern in art could be seen replicated in other fields, from physics to politics. Art could literally help us to see the world in novel ways and to break free from rigid logic. It could help us to understand how we had become separated from the world around us (animals, nature), to grasp what we had lost as that happened even as we gained the ability to see that same world more

Figure 8 Haegue Yang's Coordinates of Speculative Solidarity, 2019: https://ocula.com/art-galleries/galerie-chantal-crousel/artworks/haegue-yang/coordinates-of-speculative-solidarity/

clearly, and it could then help us to develop a more integral consciousness that would bring us back closer, once again being both part of, and apart from, the world around us, within a circle rather than just looking on in a linear way.

These analogies between art's ways of seeing and other fields can be a useful way of trying to make sense of how a civilisation thinks, and they raise a good question now. What might the arts be doing to take us beyond the aperspectival logics of the twentieth century? One candidate is what could be called a 'relational perspective': seeing things in a systemic way, as embedded in a series of relationships and connections. This is what the frontiers of thought have been grappling with – helped by ideas of complexity, systems, and evolution – and suggests a sharp swing away from the aperspectival ideas of postmodernist relativism and the multiplication of perspectives towards something that really is more integral.

A good example of this is Haegue Yang's *Coordinates of Speculative Solidarity* (Figure 8) which seeks to understand how extreme climate events might not only fracture societies but also bring them together. It's a large, digital collage, that combines satellite photos, palm leaves and storm-tracking symbols, showing the chaos of severe weather activity and suggesting how it might encourage new forms of belonging and community.

Another example is the spreading practice of 'art as research', using arts methods as a means of research rather than using other social sciences to research art.[32]

But some of the arts, at least, are lagging rather than leading. The most admired visual artists of our times – such as Gerhard Richter, Richard Serra,

Cindy Sherman, or Jasper Johns – avoid commitments, statements, anything that could be pinned down, let alone presented as systemic, while others such as Markus Lupertz or Georg Baselitz are always interesting in their play with symbols and their appropriation of art history, but, again, a world away from the frontiers of contemporary thought in other fields. The dominant twentieth-century ideal in which 'the art object itself is empty, inert; it is 'made' by the spectator.... The art is happening *because* of the canvas, but not *on* the canvas ' (the words are Marcel Duchamp's)[33] – a perfect mirror of modern orthodox economics in which all value flows from consumer preferences – protects the artist from responsibility but also perhaps from impact. This may have been an understandable reaction against the cruder variants of symbolism, where art has to be a communication, an act charged with transmissible meaning. But it is a stance which now feels dated, an ideology suited to a rampant irresponsible global capitalism but not for an era when we have to tread more lightly on the world.

Creating Slow as Well as Fast Art

Much contemporary art has become fast: it seeks to make an immediate impression, to grab the viewer in the intense competition for attention in a digital cornucopia. However, for new perspectives to have impact, we need time to absorb and digest. Here we come to an interesting, and perhaps surprising, connection between art, imagination, and memory. Recent neuroscience tells us that memory feeds imagination and vice versa.[34] We need the raw material of memories and experiences to construct plausible future scenes. But these memories have to be owned and internalised to be meaningful.

Over two thousand years ago, Socrates warned about the dangers of writing, which he feared would be the enemy of memory and thus of wisdom. He believed that true knowledge required internal memory (anamnesis) which was distinct from external memory of the kind provided by writing and from any representation which by its nature was deficient or partial (hypomnesis), because it wasn't fully absorbed.[35] So perhaps art which is merely consumed or contemplated, and litera-ture which is only read, is therefore never wholly true. It only becomes true when we have ourselves worked on it, internalised it, and absorbed it into ourselves.

It follows that art for social imagination has to be organised in ways that allow the time for it to be absorbed, adapted, and remade. In this way, it becomes, in part, an act of co-creation, rather than just an act of consumption or just an enjoyable way to pass the evening.[36] If it is just an object, just something for the passing gaze, then it is, perhaps, bound to fail, or to be nothing more than entertainment and diversion. Experiences which are shared and embodied work better.

This has to mean art that is slow. Constantin Brancusi once wrote that 'art must give suddenly, all at once, the shock of life, the sensation of breathing',[37] and we have all experienced this. Some of the greatest works achieve their effect immediately: they grab us. But to become useful to social imagination perhaps art has to be slower than this, to allow the time for thoughts to take shape.

This may be even truer of any art that aspires to a political purpose. An image can jolt or inspire. But the work of creating political change is by its nature slow, involving argument and thrashing out alternatives. It can't be sparked just by a single painting, an exhibition, or even 90 minutes in a cinema. Works of art can form part of a movement – for disability rights, radical ecology or libertarian anti-statism. But they cannot lead it.

Co-creation Not Just Consumption

The next part of the answer follows from this. For art to truly move societies, it needs to be engaged with, not just consumed. This was the conclusion Joseph Beuys reached when he wrote of the need for art to move from being passive to active, which led to his concept of 'social sculpture'. His favourite phrase, borrowed from Novalis, was that 'everyone is an artist' and the dream was to turn the whole of society into a work of art, a progressive version of Wagner's 'gesamtkunstwerk', with the public, not just the artistic genius, involved in shaping the world around them from the most everyday acts to public spaces.

One of the themes of cultural studies since the 1960s has been that culture is ubiquitous, not just the preserve of arts institutions[38] and this approach has inspired many attempts to connect the practice of art with the dynamics of social change.[39] A good example are the many projects of Umbrellium who work in cities using technology to help people rethink aspects of how it could be run, from air quality to road safety, or directly controlling public digital sculptures through tablets. These projects are deliberately participatory – they involve many people in observation and creation, and they are, most of the time, fun.

Another example is Collusion (shown below, Figure 9) who used big projections and social media to bring the people of a town – Kings Lynn in the east of England – into a conversation about its future. The idea was to combine multiple elements – from personal stories to spectacular shows, and from small-scale cabins to large events with thousands of people on the streets – to weave together a story about possible futures.

My home town, Luton, used the 2019 centenary of a riot that burnt down the town hall in a similar way. The riot had been started by veterans from the First

Figure 9 Collusion installation, Kings Lynn, 2017: www.collusion.org.uk/pro
jects/kings-lynn-rd-challenge/

World War. After years in the trenches seeing mass slaughter around them, they had returned home to find a country with high unemployment and little if any help for them to find housing or income. That day, the town's elite were due to hold a grand dinner in the town hall to celebrate the end of the war, although most of them had contributed little. The veterans became ever more angry, and ever more drunk, until they broke into the town hall and burned it to the ground. A century later, the aim was to use this half-forgotten memory to prompt a conversation about the town's past, present, and future, with theatre, music, social media, and video as prompts (pictured in Figure 10). The town's makeup had changed dramatically – with a majority from non-UK backgrounds and roughly a third Muslim. But this act of rebellion opened up a very different view of history to the official stories of royalty and castles, empire and victory.

Promising experiments have also used technologies to generate physical, embodied experiences of different kinds of shared reality. Most cultures have used dance, and sometimes ecstatic dance, to help us connect to each other (sometimes helped by alcohol or drugs).[40] But now such experiences can be designed, hacked, and rearranged, helping us to feel connections, or tensions, in novel ways that just watching or hearing cannot. Ghislaine Boddington has been one of the pioneers of these approaches, using dance and physical motion in space to help people feel in their bodies different ways of organising society.[41]

Engagement in the making of art using all of these different methods may be becoming second nature for a growing proportion of the population who want to take part as well as observe. A generation ago, New Zealand scientist James Flynn showed that IQ levels were rising all over the world. He showed that a

Figure 10 Luton Town Hall lit up during the People Power Passion Peace Day Riots anniversary spectacular. Photo credit: Luton Council, 2019

large part of this involved the growing ability to think hypothetically, in abstractions and in the generation of new categories. This was partly the result of the more stimulating visual environments of modern life which have allowed a 'liberation from the concrete', that has changed how we think and see. But it also expands the population who are at ease with creativity, including conceptual creativity.

Hacking as Ethos and Method

I've already mentioned hacking and see the hacker movement as an important influence on the arts both directly and indirectly. It suggests an ethos for linking creativity and imagination that runs counter to the nineteenth- or twentieth-century ideals of the genius artist, from whose head profound truths emanate, offering instead an approach that fiddles, adjusts, deconstructs, and reconstructs things that are already lying around, bricolage rather than grand design.

As an ethos, and a way of working, hacking in its modern sense emerged at MIT in the 1950s and 1960s and promoted work done for curiosity rather than reward; a belief in sharing and openness; and faith in decentralisation and bettering the world. The movement, described by the writer Stephen Levy as a 'new way of life, with a philosophy, an ethic and a dream', proved hugely influential.[42] It provided an ideology for the open-source movement whose technologies underpin much of the Internet, and it continues to offer an alternative vision, both to the surveillance capitalism of Facebook and Google, and to the way digital technologies are used by governments like China's as a tool for control.[43]

It can be applied to almost anything. In the arts, it encourages the spread of pop-ups and galleries of unfinished works and ideas (for example, there's one in Johannesburg). Applied to public parks, it opens up options for rethinking spaces, turning flowerbeds into allotments for food; allowing primary schools or groups of the elderly to become curators; opening up for music, festivals, or restaurants. Helsinki's much-copied 'restaurant day' is a good example of this hacking: specified days when the normal rules would be suspended so that anyone could sell food anywhere. Freed from constraints, thousands of people create pop-up restaurants, often in public parks, embodying a vision of a more active, creative society.

Homes can be hacked too – with changed uses for rooms, roofs, or entrances – creatively disrupting the original vision of the planner and architect. The spirit is of learning by doing; feeling our way to new possibilities in steps rather than through grand visions.

This hacker ethos confirms a broader point about originality. Dig beneath the surface of the utopias, philosophies, and model communities and you quickly find that their creators have drawn on existing themes and ideas. Ideas never come from nowhere. They are always extensions, graftings, or inversions of things that are already present in the world (in a later section, I go into more detail about exactly how this process works): bricolage as much as brilliance.

There is, of course, a continuum from creative inspiration to pure plagiarism: and the tendency of film and TV towards remakes, sequels, and prequels can be a sign of waning creativity (and the dulling constraints of business models that rely on audiences knowing what they are about to receive). But some reuse is simply how culture works, whether in film, music, or literature: the greatest composers and writers play with existing elements, codes, and grammars. Recognising this doesn't diminish our admiration. But it does qualify the classic ideal of the individual artist as prophet.

4 The Forms: How Can They Explore the Future?

The previous section was suggestive of the approach that the arts might take to engage with social change – focused on perspectives, co-creation, hacking. Now in this section, I look at how different art forms can and might engage with social imagination, focusing in particular on film and television, architecture, and technology. But I start with something that is not quite an art form, the art of campaigning.

Politics, Campaigns, and Provocation

I've already suggested how problematic it is that so much of art has become integrated into the lifestyle of the ultra-rich, allied with luxury, fashion, and

Figure 11 Robert E. Lee monument in Richmond, Virginia, after graffiti.
Source: Mk17b, CC BY-SA 4.0, via Wikimedia Commons

excessive consumption, blunting artists' ability to offer critique except in very 'safe' and unthreatening ways, or in a superficial postmodern irony that never draws any blood.

But there are many exceptions who have used art to disrupt, embarrass, and challenge power and wealth in their new forms. A striking example was the transformation of the public statue of Robert E. Lee in Richmond, Virginia (Figure 11), by activists of Black Lives Matter, leaving it covered with a growing forest of slogans and the names of victims of police violence, part of a global rethinking of the roles of statues and museums.

Another is the work of Forensic Architecture challenging the role of the then vice-chair of the Witney Museum over his company's role in making tear gas, a rare recent example of challenging elite power in the art market.

Art has also become a place for ever more sophisticated critique and dissection of power. Kate Crawford's fascinating project on the Amazon Echo (now at MOMA and pictured in Figure 12) is a good, didactic example, revealing the material and data flows that lie behind AI.

This spirit of art as campaigning can be found in formal politics too. Mayor Antanas Mockus was a striking example, using mime artists and painted outlines of bodies to shift public behaviour in his city of Bogota. In each of these examples, the campaigning itself becomes a work of art, a fusion of medium and message. It may still be stronger as critique, or bearing witness, than as design or proposal. But it does help to shift the world along by transforming awareness, revealing hidden and ignored structures of power and oppression.

Famous artists can use their fame to campaign and shame – as Picasso did in the Spanish Civil War and Bono and Bob Geldof did on debt, and many others on issues ranging from climate change to abortion laws. But politics can also be a predator when it comes to culture: using and misusing. Luis Fonsi complained about the use of his song 'Despacito' by Maduro in Venezuela[44] while Bruce Springsteen and Neil Young were just two of the many US musicians who complained about the use of their songs by Donald Trump at his rallies.[45] Artworks, once loose in the world, are harder for their creators to control.

Utopias: Fiction, Film, and Television and the Frontiers of Social Change

Fiction should be able to cope more easily with social imagination than other art forms. It can describe in detail possible future societies, and there is a long history of fictional utopias and imagined worlds. These have provided a space for conflicting visions, albeit skewed towards the literate, prosperous, and time-rich (as Chinua Achebe put it, 'until the lions have their own historians, the history of the hunt will always glorify the hunter.')

Over the last five or more centuries, many fictional utopias have straddled the worlds of culture and social imagination, usually written by the privileged. Famous examples include Thomas More's *Utopia* and the work of Tommaso Campanella who, in 1602, wrote from prison a description of a virtuous, theocratic utopia in his book *The City of the Sun*. It portrayed a city with shared goods, a four-hour working day, and special praise for those who had to work hardest, such as the builders. The walls of the city were painted with the best of the arts and knowledge – an encyclopedia in physical form.

Feminism was foreshadowed in extraordinary early works like Christine de Pisan's fifteenth century work *The Book of the City of Ladies* and seventeenth-century English scientist Margaret Cavendish's *Blazing World*, a proto–science

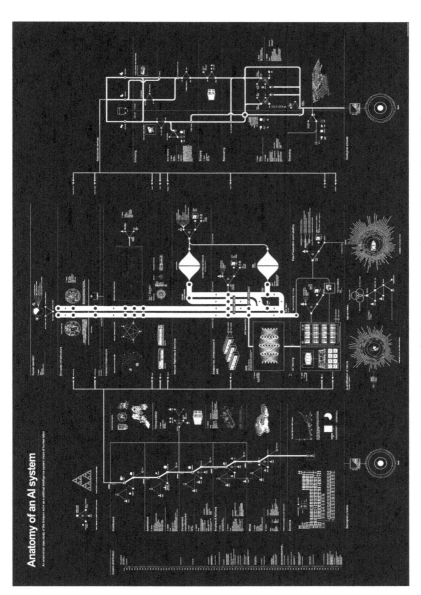

Figure 12 From Kate Crawford, on Amazon Echo, at MOMA, New York

fiction utopia (oddly, like Pisan's, full of talking animals). A century later, Sarah Scott, an English novelist and reformer, wrote *Millennium Hall*, which offered a feminist 'bluestocking' utopia of education and improvement, with, again, property held in common. None of these directly prompted moves to give women the vote, or anything else. But they played their part in slowly undermining the assumptions of patriarchy.

In the nineteenth century, literary utopias proliferated. Some were best-sellers like Edward Bellamy's *Looking Backward: 2000–1887* (published in 1888) which became one of the three best-selling books of all time in the United States. It described how the United States was transformed by a peaceful revolution that abolished private property and taxes, saw professions like lawyers and soldiers disappear, and enabled retirement at 45. In it, we can also find references to everyday innovations like home deliveries and credit cards.

The utopian literary tradition continued through the twentieth century. In her book *The Dispossessed* (1974), the speculative fiction writer Ursula LeGuin described in detail the dynamics of Annares, an anarchist-communitarian world, while Octavia Butler, founder of Afrofuturism, used fiction to travel in time both to the past, to the age of slavery, and to possible futures, after nuclear war, with parasitic insects or with a character struggling with hyper-empathy, feeling the pain of everyone near her, and ultimately creating a new community.

Utopias show up in other art forms too. One of the most intriguing was Drexciya – the idea of an African American group in Detroit in the 1970s who imagined an underwater country populated by the unborn children of pregnant African women who were thrown off slave ships. The babies had adapted to breathe underwater in their mothers' wombs and had created a utopian society at the bottom of the ocean, sparking a feast of imaginative visuals and music, a parallel to the contemporary work by George Clinton who created science fiction funk visions, steeped in black culture and offering a counterpoint to the stiff, white, conservative sci-fi orthodoxy of figures like Robert Heinlein.

Oddly, though, such fictional utopias have almost completely disappeared, pushed out by dystopian warnings of what lies ahead. This is a shame because they play a useful role in helping to warm people up to alternative possibilities. Immersion in a possible world liberates us from the illusion that the world is natural or fixed.

Yet the literalness of utopias can also be a limitation. They are often too complete to be convincing and very few had much direct influence on the world. Their influence came more often at a tangent, opening up ways of thinking and introducing new concepts. Even though they often offered specific designs, these were almost never taken up. Indeed, the more didactic or literal they were, the less influence they had.

For film and television, the choices are different. Film has a rich history of dystopian portrayal, including some truly great films like *Metropolis*. But it has no examples of convincing utopias. The same is true of television.

Yet TV can normalise new ways of thinking and its biggest effects can come from making new ideas and attitudes seem natural. It portrayed black (and indeed female) US presidents well ahead of reality (e.g. the series *24*) and prepared audiences for pandemics through films like Steven Soderbergh's *Contagion*.

After all, the status quo reinforces itself as imaginary, and as apparently natural, through repetition, not through overt propaganda. It's subtly woven into the background of daily life, the assumptions of the workplace, family or politics, TV or news. A similar approach is necessary for change – through equally subliminal action that makes new ideas seem simply obvious or natural, as has happened to attitudes to sexuality or race, veganism or recycling. Messages that are too overt by contrast risk being ignored or resented.

TV can also influence social imagination through its forms as much as its content. Over the last two decades, TV story lines have become ever more complex, interwoven, and ambiguous, as well as longer, as more sophisticated audiences have become better able to juggle multiple characters all in motion. It's no longer necessary for everything to be explained; tied up; closed down. Multiple perspectives can be held in tension. Here we see both a cause and an effect of the rising levels of conceptual reasoning in IQ that may make it easier to grasp a plural, multidimensional future.

But the problem for TV and film is that they cannot easily escape being literal, and their very literalness – showing every building, piece of clothing, or means of transport – renders them oddly less effective as a vehicle for imagination than the novel, or audio, which leaves much of this work to the reader or listener.

The growing body of artworks addressing climate change confirms the point. While film can be a powerful tool for warning, the novel may be better placed to handle the nuances of a profound transition than other forms.[46] What one author called 'socio-climatic imaginaries' can be found in novels such as Paolo Bacigalupi's *The Water Knife* and Kim Stanley Robinson's *Green Earth* (both from 2015), and Stanley Robinson's later *The Ministry for the Future* (2020), which go beyond the eco-apocalypse to examine the multiple interactions between nature and social organisation. Stanley Robinson has spoken of science fiction as 'a kind of future-scenarios modelling, in which some course of history is pursued as a thought experiment, starting from now and moving some distance off into the future' and makes a good case that literature is better placed to do this than anything else.[47]

His work is admirable, but very much an exception. Few novelists have bothered to collaborate with experts to picture the possible future of care for the elderly or transport planning. Some do take the trouble to talk to scientists and technologists. But the quality of social imagination tends to be much lower than imagination about future hardware.

So perhaps we should see the role of literature less in terms of offering utopias, designs, and detailed scenarios and more in terms of sensing deep trends. There is at least a long history of sensing of this kind – from fragments of the many utopias discussed earlier to famous novels like HG Wells' *The World Set Free*, published in 1914, which described atomic bombs contaminating battlefields, or George Orwell's *1984* which predicted a totalitarian one-party state with telescreens judging people by facial expressions and heart rate – something that contemporary China is fast making a reality. Other examples include Arthur C Clarke's suggestion of geostationary orbits and Isaac Asimov's work on the ethics and rules that might govern robots, or Nicola Griffith's writing (*Ammonite*) on a world where most men have been wiped out. Less well-known examples include John Brunner's novel *Stand on Zanzibar*, which imagined a powerful European Union, a resurgent China, the decay of industrial cities like Detroit and the election of a 'President Obomi', or Jovan Radulović's 1983 play *Dove Hole*, about an Ustashe massacre against their Serbian neighbours, a notion which quickly became reality as the Yugoslav civil wars wreaked havoc.

All of these examples confirm that writers of literature can sometimes sense what's on the horizon, though often messily and chaotically rather than in neat lines. Yet it's still not quite clear what the reader or viewer does next: is engagement with the cultural artefact a prompt to action, or is it enough just to raise awareness? In principle, it must be good to promote inspiring examples of change.[48] But this may not be enough to prompt change; it may just provide confirmation for the already converted.

Amitav Ghosh complained that writing on climate change was classed as science fiction: 'It is as though in the literary imagination climate change were somehow akin to extra-terrestrials or interplanetary travel.'[49] Yet half a century ago, Ursula LeGuin described science fiction as an ideal training for the imagination, since it encourages writers and readers to imagine – what if this, what if that – acclimatising us to possible futures and challenging the assumption that there is something inevitable about the way things are.[50]

Social Media and Data

What then of the dominant media of the twenty-first century – the social media of TikTok and Twitter, Facebook and WeChat? Forty years ago, Neil Postman warned of a culture that was 'amusing itself to death', with television replacing the fixed structures of the written word with 'sequencing of information so random, so disparate in scale and value, as to be incoherent, even psychotic'.[51] This might be an even more accurate description of what came after television, the data-driven social media that mobilised the self, its experiences, and presentations, as a fuel for the economy.

These platforms in principle make it easier to organise; easier to share. The fifteen-second formats of TikTok have allowed millions to be creators, ignoring any past hierarchies of judgement about what counts as art, or what counts as good. They have taken further the long-term trends to democratise creative production.

Moreover, unlike TV and film, these social media mobilise a collective judgement far more quickly than ever before in history. They can both support virtual lynch-mobs but also a more progressive questioning of the assumptions of the privileged. The #MeToo and Black Lives Matter movements are perhaps the clearest examples of this collective moral sense, which older writers and artists, brought up to believe in their autonomy and lack of accountability, find hard to stomach.

Yet the economic base of the platforms is paradoxical in this sense. It is both hyper-individualistic, reaching ever deeper in the very nature of the self, but also social and collective, valuing the self only insofar as it is socially valued by the interest, likes, and shares of others. So, although it is easier than ever to collect a group together to work, create, or imagine, such initiatives operate in tension with some of the DNA of the platforms, a DNA that is based on the harvesting of data in order to sell products and services.

Indeed, because the language of social media is identity (as is its economy – a represented identity made up of data on past actions, that mirrors the experienced identity of the individual), this also becomes the language of politics: any issue becomes framed through what it means for identity rather than, for example, interests or common beliefs. This favours surfaces over interiors, expression over insight, attitude over accuracy. Authenticity, or the ability to fake authenticity, comes to be valued, as does the ability to belong to a group. Activism comes to be about activating identities as much as changing minds.

All of these tendencies, which are encouraged by the character of a more data-driven economy, may tend to preclude imagination or the longer time horizons of fundamental social change. Our mediums may be becoming the enemies of our future. What appears to be our new public sphere is in some respects stacked against our ability to behave as a public that can imagine and shape its own destiny.[52]

How Architecture Feeds Imagination, and the Paradoxes of Visibility

Architecture has a unique place in the relationship between art and social imagination. Architects can literally show a new way of living – convivial workspaces or housing; buildings that mimic nature and reintegrate city and ecology; grand towers that project power and glory.

But their very ability to crystallise a social vision also makes their work paradoxical. They always risk promoting the illusion that the physical alone shapes the social: that if we could only build a city in a new way, a more benign society would follow (a position sometimes described as 'architectural determinism').[53]

Instead, this thesis has been repeatedly disproven. There are many examples of building projects that were expected to lead to social improvements but which failed to do so. Yet subsequently small changes, or social adjustments, made them liveable and attractive. In this way the projects disproved their own premise. The invisible shaped them as much as the visible.

A very common example of this was the proliferation of tower blocks in the 1950s and 1960s, influenced by Le Corbusier and others. His plans for the Ville Contemporaine, an idealised model city for three million people, based on identical sixty-storey-tall apartment buildings surrounded by lower zig-zag apartment blocks and a large park where residents would live and work, were captured in his book *Towards an Architecture*. The inspiration came from machines and factories and he believed that the future ideal would be 'to go to work in the superb office of a modern factory, rectangular and well-lit, painted in white ... where healthy activity and laborious optimism reign'.[54]

His ideas generated plans for many cities – from Rio de Janeiro to Algiers. Some were built – notably Chandigargh in India and a workers' suburb in Bordeaux, and some of his design concepts have aged well. His visions appeared to offer more space, and an easy integration of work and neighbourhood. They claimed to offer a complete view of life – of how families would live and how people would thrive – and were taken up with enthusiasm by the social engineer architects of the Soviet Union partly for that reason. They could be built fast and gave families more space than the tenements they replaced.

But it soon became clear that the picture of how societies work was more abstract than empirical, more idealised than practical. His designs deduced how people should live rather than observing how they chose to live. The designs of Le Corbusier and his followers often disrupted the social networks, particularly those in extended families, that were so vital to communities before. This was a pattern well documented in Michael Young and Peter Wilmott's *Family and Kinship in East London*, which in turn influenced the writings of Jane Jacobs and others who came to see Corbusier's heirs as the enemies of city life, not their friend. Soon the places they built became unpopular, associated with crime, conflict, and neglect. A generation later, adjustments helped them recover: these included concierges, gated entrances, and carefully organised security – all changes that were invisible in the architects' designs but turned out to be vital to human needs. Recent research on the impact of built environments on suicide confirms the point: they do appear to have an effect, but it's mainly through how safe people feel, which in turn is shaped by many invisible factors (such as how many neighbours they know by name) as well as visible ones.[55]

The opposite example was the garden city, the brainchild of Ebenezer Howard who was a rare combination of anarchist *and* planner. Horrified by the unhealthy and unhappy cities of Victorian England, he came up with the idea of garden cities – partly inspired by Edward Bellamy's novel *Looking Backward*. Garden cities would solve the problems of congestion and high land prices by moving the population out to new places where they would live and work, surrounded by countryside and clean air. His vision cleverly looked forward to the future *and* back to an imagined past where people lived a more organic way of life. The goal was a society that would be 'neither capitalistic nor bureaucratic-socialistic: a society based on voluntary cooperation among men and women, working and living in small self-governing commonwealths'.[56] Nor were these only words. Ebenezer Howard was a rare visionary who was also practical (much of his original book set out financial calculations showing why the garden cities offered such a good return to investors) and, after his first success in Letchworth in England, hundreds were set up around the world.

His cities have generally succeeded. But they didn't succeed as he imagined. Most ended up as pleasant commuter suburbs rather than integrating work and home. Again, the visible aspects of the designs couldn't grasp the invisible networks of economics and social interactions.

More recent examples like the radical eco-town in Freiburg or the surveillance capitalism of Google's Sidewalk Labs plans for Toronto (which fell apart in 2020) also clearly embody very different social imaginaries. So does Vienna's Frauen-Werk-Stadt, built in the 1990s, a rare example of architecture created for and by women, offering a very different picture of how cities could work, allowing easy supervision of children, low-rise accessibility, and plenty of gardens and roofs for play.

Figure 13 Andras Gyorfi, TSI,
http://seasteading.org/design-contest-winners, this image is CCA

Incheon's New Song-Do is another, almost opposite example, integrating high-tech surveillance into its technocratic ideal of the future city: safe, neat, ordered, but soulless. If nothing else, they are good prompts for forcing us to think about what kinds of cities we would like to live in (the people of Toronto decided, on reflection, that the Google version was not for them).

The individualist equivalent is summed up in the various 'sea-steading' projects that aim to create libertarian utopias offshore. Figure 13 shows one of the proposed designs for these 'seasteads'. Others that are even more individualistic in spirit include Ocean Builders' 'Seapods', designed for a single household, which neatly sum up their philosophy which privileges the independent individual (the pictures are less clear on where their energy comes from or where their waste goes, not to mention their dependence on distant sources of food, spare parts, and just about everything else).

In architecture, there is a long history of attempts to fuse a social and an aesthetic ideal, for example, in the work of the Italian group Archizoom,[57] denouncing soulless functionality, or the many attempts to design buildings that are more ecological and biomimetic, and less anthropocentric, such as the recent image bank created by a group of Finnish architects to help the transition to a net-zero society. The very physicality of buildings can make it easier to play with alternative imaginary futures – like Mogadishu 2030, a project for artists to imagine how that city, victim of some of the worst misfortunes of the late twentieth and early twenty-first centuries, could evolve.[58]

More recently architects have used their skill for advocacy and investigation, notably in the work of Forensic Architecture's investigations of human rights abuses in Israel and China. Their methods use data, 3D reconstructions, audio, social media, and maps to dissect the wrongs of the world, turning art galleries into places that engage with the troubles of the world rather than escaping from them.

Here visual engineering, and the design of virtual worlds, is used as a way of seeing rather than as a way of designing. This at least is one route for architecture, pioneered by brilliant figures such as Alison Killing, but again bearing witness rather than proposing.

By contrast, the more design-oriented projects always remind us of the ambiguity in imagination. The visual nature of architectural designs makes them ideal tools for thinking about new kinds of society: whether proposing vertical farming and localised food production or housing that includes care and social supports for the elderly. But too precise a vision for a community or a city leaves less space for people to make their own history, and their own cities. Often the best designs are deliberately incomplete or self-effacing. Taking this idea further, Buckminster Fuller, for example, proposed 'Dymaxion Houses' (Figure 14) – round structures weighing only three tons (rather than the typical home's one hundred) and promised that architecture should 'sublimate' itself, making itself invisible while providing simple shelters that provided security from the weather rather than screaming out the architect's ego. He never quite

Figure 14 Buckminster Fuller, Dymaxion Houses. Image courtesy of the Estate of R. Buckminster Fuller.

got them to work (his geodesic domes were much more successful) but the idea remains intriguing.[59]

More recent examples in a similar spirit are Wikihouse, a repository of open-source designs, and Finland's Y Foundation projects on vertical parks for the homeless, that reuse containerisation to allow very flexible, and low-carbon, buildings where each element and function can be replaced. Rem Koolhaas' recent attempts to imagine rural futures in a physical form have a comparable ethos.[60] These avoid the risks of overly perfect blueprints that are to be imposed on a grateful population. Instead, they offer elements, building blocks in both a metaphorical and literal sense, that others can combine and adapt to their own needs. Here too we see an architecture less dominated by the starchitects – the global superstars concerned for buildings to burnish their reputations – and instead an architecture that can be better integrated with the practice of social imagination, design, and experiment, closer to hacking than blueprints.

Winston Churchill was right to comment that we shape buildings and that they then shape us. But they are not the only thing that shapes us and rarely the most important. The humbler architects try to remember this simple fact.

How Art Can Play on the Technology Frontiers

Art has always been defined by technology as well as playing its part in defining the frontiers of technology. In the pre-modern world, the cutting edge of technologies for water, fire, or metalwork were often developed for entertainment not utility, and later equivalents were mobilised to help with extravagant displays for kings and emperors.

Something similar is happening today with the vast river of digital hardware and software that now includes data, social media, the Internet of Things, AI, artificial life, blockchain, quantum, holography, augmented and virtual reality (AR and VR), avatars and haptics, swarms, drones, biohacking, 3D printing, and many others, all providing mediums for artists as well as topics to explore. The CGI methods pioneered by the huge studios of George Lucas in California and Peter Jackson in New Zealand, for example, blur any distinction between reality and fantasy while the games pioneered by studios like Rockstar North in Edinburgh, home to the Grand Theft Auto series, or Fortnite, allow players to wander and explore, transforming our relationship to narrative. Immersion becomes an ideal rather than just passive viewing – with works like Punchdrunk's *Sleep No More* as exemplars alongside the many hybrids of living people and generated images. In other words, the frontiers of technology can, in the arts, also be frontiers of perception and social imagination.

I've long been interested in how we might push on the artistic, social, and technological frontiers simultaneously, applying R&D models to the arts themselves. I oversaw one fund to support this kind of systematic experimentation when I worked at Nesta, particularly designed to encourage creative experiment around emerging technologies like AI, VR, and AR. We could find very few precedents for systematic funding for R&D, and often little knowledge in the arts world about how to design experiments that could generate more general knowledge. The fund sought out partnerships of arts organisations, tech firms, and researchers to test out new uses of technology – sometimes to enhance the relationship with audiences and to raise revenues but also to advance art forms themselves. Over fifty projects were supported covering a range of fields, from uses of mobile phones to data, and with many looking at potential new business models.

Examples included the 'talking statues' around the UK which used a QR code (Figure 15), and recorded pieces from actors, to bring hundreds of old statues alive (shortly before the Black Lives Matter movement precipitated much more vigorous debate about the meaning and legitimacy of so many of the statues that filled up city centres). Another project worked with the Holocaust Museum to capture in holograms the memories of holocaust survivors in an interactive

Figure 15 Talking plaque for Holmes statue. Professorclee, CC BY-SA 4.0, via Wikimedia Commons

format. Others used new haptic tools for theatre, opening it up to people with impaired sight and hearing.

We weren't successful in persuading the main arts funders to make R&D a normal part of their work, though I suspect that this will come in time. But the programme did lead to a significant allocation of funds from the government's Industrial Strategy to support R&D around immersive technologies, the first time that the arts had been properly integrated into broader support for technology R&D.

This is at least one way for the arts to engage in actively shaping the future: using, bending and adapting emerging technologies, and perhaps preparing us for a world of AI producing cultural products on an industrial scale, connected objects moving in tandem; or city squares re-animated with light, and responsive imagery.

Experiments of this kind help the arts explore tangential connections, like Christian Bök's experiments writing poetry into bacterial DNA, or Eduardo Kac encoding parts of the book of Genesis into Morse code, DNA, and then into bacteria culture, which was meant to spark new thoughts about genetic modification and how we store information, as well as the fuzzy boundaries between what's natural and what's artificial. By working on the frontiers in this way, the arts make technology both more human and more strange.

Frontiers of Perception in Art and Science

I started this Element by talking about perspective: how we see the world both literally and metaphorically. Our ability to imagine depends on an ability to see things: the word 'imagine' refers to images, so it is appropriate to investigate how the picturing of things and the picturing of a possible new society could be related.

It might be thought that theories precede perceptions. But history suggests otherwise. Repeatedly in the history of science, a new way of seeing things later prompted new hypotheses and theories. Telescopes made it possible to understand the movements of stars and planets. Microscopes showed the teeming life existing at a microscopic scale. The microscope, X-rays, and electron microscopes each opened up new perspectives on the world, by revealing a new kind of reality and then prompting the formulation of theories and hypotheses. For example, the achromatic-lens microscope developed in the 1820s by Joseph Lister led directly to germ theory, which many consider the most important breakthrough in medicine before 1900.

In our own time, the CERN collider has given us new insights into the world of minute particles and prompted a succession of artists to visualise its strange patterns. A recent example is the Mexican artist Tania Candiani exploring the connections between quantum physics and indigenous knowledge. In parallel, our knowledge of the macroscopic and cosmic scales of space and time have been transformed by the images from the Hubble space telescope, generating pictures that have a strange beauty, simultaneously reinforcing our smallness in the universe but also oddly making it feel more like a home.

Much of social imagination depends on seeing things in fresh ways. In the mid-nineteenth century, John Snow had mapped patterns of cholera infections around a pump in Broad Street in central London. He showed that the infections had all come from the same source, and by revealing something new about how the city worked, laid the foundations for modern public health (and for how we track pandemics). In a similar way, the statistical method of measuring poverty paved the way for the welfare state. (As Bertrand Russell was reputed to have said, the mark of a civilised human is the ability to 'look at a column of numbers, and weep.'[61]) The sociologist Emile Durkheim's famous study of suicide in late nineteenth century France showed how a phenomenon that appeared very personal was better understood as influenced by large social forces in ways that could be mapped with statistics.[62]

In economics, the ability to see 'externalities' or waste transforms how we think about the ways economies work. Once you have seen a diagram of the discarded materials from production processes, the wasted energy and unrecycled materials when things have been discarded, you can never view economies in quite the same way again. I learned economics at a time when none of this was measured, mapped, or talked about, and when economics helped to reinforce the still-unresolved vices of an industrial system that was profligate in its wastefulness.

Today's breakthroughs in social imagination are also likely to be sparked by new ways of seeing. For example, a recent study of domestic homicide in the UK showed that the best predictor was a suicide attempt or talk of suicide by the perpetrator – an insight that opens up a radically different way of seeing the risks of murder and trying to prevent it. Much more detailed measurement of psychological well-being is opening up new ways of thinking about society that complements the dominant economic metrics of GDP, income, and wealth, showing, for example, how the experience of debt worsens stress, which in turn damages cognitive capacity and IQ and leads people to make worse choices.

This data can be made beautiful, and a striking feature of our times is the quality of work on the boundaries of statistics, computer graphics, and aesthetics: rendering the complex patterns of social phenomena in ways that are exciting, pleasing, stunning, often showing subtle variegations quite different from the aggregate statistics of the twentieth century. This, surely, is a new art form and one that prepares us to imagine quite new patterns and relationships.

I hope the numerous examples I've given in this section give a flavour of the many ways in which different art forms can engage with what we see, what we understand, and what we can change. In the next section I want to go up a gear – to look in more detail at the kind of society we might wish to live in and what art might mean in that world.

5 Collective Consciousness

If humanity is to have a future, and to survive the threats of climate change and environmental destruction, then the hope must be that we progress to a more advanced form of consciousness. The Internet has given us intimations of this more connected, more aware consciousness. But it is only that – a hint, not a blueprint.

What it hints at is a world where we are radically more aware of those around us, their hopes, feelings, and fears, and radically more connected to the natural world on which we depend too.

That picture is plausible, if difficult, with the arts both providing guides to this future and also preparing to play a more central role in this more advanced society where the ability to create and shape is widely distributed, where social creativity is natural: a world where art does not sit outside society looking in but is rather embedded within it.

In this section, I investigate how we might think about the relationship of art to a more evolved collective consciousness of this kind. I look at the long-term trends in values and ways of thinking. I show how methods for creativity could become much more widespread, and how these can cut across music or painting or social change. I then turn to what I call a dialectical mentality, how we can make the most of the time that may be liberated later in this century, and how we can learn to say goodbye to things that have served humans well but have now outlived their purpose.

Seeing Ourselves in Time

Let me start with time. Any imaginative ideas about the future either explicitly or implicitly take a view of time. It may be seen as potentially progressive, with the promise that our children and grandchildren may live better lives than us. Or we may assume that things move in cyclical ways or even that we are condemned to long-term decline. We can assume that things will change fast or that they'll move slowly.

There is no reliable science of the pace of change, which is why experts are constantly surprised, just like the rest of us.

The arts can help fill this space, opening up our awareness of time, and the tensions between the biographical time we live in, the historical time we observe, and the cosmic time which is so far beyond our comprehension. They can help us to see our present as a past, seen through the possible eyes of the future.

But perhaps their greatest value is to free us from the tyranny of linear time. In art, as in dreams, time is squashed, stretched, and emptied out. Television and film can play with flashbacks, reverse time, or mashed up time. Everything can be simultaneous. In art, anything can be remade or reimagined. In society, it often feels like the opposite. Indeed, the social world is reified – it comes to be seen as a thing, and natural, resistant to any change – whereas art can protect us from this 'fallacy of reification', of seeing things as more fixed than they really are.

Connecting art to society automatically helps us to see the world as more plastic, more malleable – it restores our agency. Of course, there are limits: the world is never a blank canvas. But that is where other skills come in, those of the economists, psychologists; experts in organisation and engineers who can always provide reasons why something is impossible. We need the creative, artistic sensibility to help us see what might, just, be possible.

Values and Consciousness

One of the things that might be possible is a very different kind of humanity. For the last thirty years many detailed studies of global values have told a broadly optimistic story of how values are changing as people move away from primary concerns over scarcity or survival towards valuing self-expression and freedom. They show a slow but steady movement away from traditional values to more rational and secular values. This deep, long-term trend correlates closely with economic prosperity and the presence of a healthy democracy. It's not universal and in countries where median incomes have stagnated for several decades (like the United States), or where democracy has been stunted (like Russia), the trend is much less clear-cut.

Christoph Welzel, who works on the World Values Survey, sees in these trends a global spread of emancipation, fed by the universal human desire to live free from external constraints.[63] According to this view, when the main existential constraints on life have been removed, people become more interested in freedom and direct their energies into social movements and the fight against discrimination of all kinds. His argument also suggests that some parts of the world – those with relatively cold climates and seas, and low incidence of infectious disease – have been able to move more quickly in this direction than others, suggesting a rough geography of emancipatory imagination that's very different from the geography of the first civilisations or states that grew up in much hotter climates.

Welzel's views echo those of many others who have tried to make sense of how consciousness evolves. All social progress involves changes in how we see, think, and feel, as well as progress in institutions. In the past, that led us to radically transform our views of violence and honour; of slavery and sexuality. It allowed us to empathise with strangers and to grasp the dynamics of complex ecosystems like the world's climate. To realise, that, in the words of Gwendolyn Brooks, 'we are each other's harvest, we are each other's business; we are each other's magnitude and bonds'.[64]

In one view of the future, consciousness will continue to evolve in these directions – beyond identifying with the tribe or nation to identify not just with humanity as a whole but with the whole biosphere, so that we become part of a truly collective consciousness and intelligence. The most exciting accounts of social imagination emphasise just how much our grandchildren may think in radically different ways to us. These ideas can be found in the writings of the followers of Jean Gebser, such as Clare Graves and Ken Wilber, and many other accounts of a hierarchy of consciousness that is taking us away from the particular attachments of tribe, nation, or religion towards a more universal and integrated consciousness.[65]

I've written elsewhere about what this consciousness might look and how it might spread unevenly, to be found at first only in small, marginal pockets that will be rich in art, and rich in wild, expansive imagination, as well as rich in new ways of being as well as new ways of doing. Perhaps this is what the European Union is trying to support with its ideas for a new European Bauhaus, purporting to see a renaissance in consciousness that links circularity in the economy, radical democracy, and the empowerment and expression offered by digital platforms.[66]

But such ideas will also have to contend with powerful opponents and the twenty-first century may be defined as much by new clashes as by potential progress. The most important alternatives to a more advanced consciousness are authoritarian expressions of technological nationalism which are already enjoying a revival through leaders like Modi, Erdogan, Salvini, and Bolsonaro. Their most significant exemplar today is, perhaps ironically, a communist, Xi Jinping, since Xi Jinping–thought is now an official part of the Chinese constitution and promises a Chinese dream to compete with the American dream. This thought is vague about what the 21st century might bring, but it's suggestive of a glorious future of national success, technological triumph, and opportunities for the mass of the population, that has more in common with the frontiers of the late nineteenth century than the frontiers of thought and consciousness in the twenty-first.

It also takes a stand on art. In the words of a speech by Xi Jinping in 2015:

> contemporary arts must take patriotism as a theme, leading the people to establish and maintain correct views of history, nationality, statehood, and culture while firmly building up the integrity and confidence of the Chinese people .... When it comes to outstanding works of art, it is best if they first achieve success in terms of ideology.

Much of the speech from which this quote is taken was an attack on the market, echoing many conservative critics of vulgarity in the West. But it also warned against any focus on the 'dark side of society' and too much interest in foreign ideas.

Here we see a hardening authoritarianism that's increasingly visible around the world, and that's likely to be intolerant of any arts that challenge the powerful, squeezing out the space for dissent or mockery, let alone bearing witness to the harms committed by all-powerful states.

So values and consciousness may evolve – but they may also be shaped by battles with older ways of thinking, and everyone will have to decide where they stand. The values-free stances of the twentieth century, refusing any commitment, any stance, may look painfully inadequate in such a context.

Spreading Universal Tools for Creativity on the Boundaries of Social Change and the Arts

All of the visions of a more advanced individual and collective consciousness emphasise creativity, and an ideal where more of our lives are creative in every sense, from daily life and relationships to the society around us.

I have long been interested in some of the grammars of creativity that likewise seem to be common across multiple domains, though they are much more commonly attended to in fields that are self-consciously creative, like design or the visual arts. These could become much more common and everyday, and one vision of a more autopoietic society with an advanced consciousness emphasises the idea of constant creation and recreation in every aspect of social life. That creativity can use the common grammars of creativity: extending, grafting, adding, subtracting, inverting, and randomising.

In relation to music, for example, each of these has a logic, such as extending a particular approach, like Bach producing a fugue with six instead of three parts. Grafting might mean adding in an old folk tune to an orchestral piece. Adding might mean including an additional instrument. Inverting might mean putting the melody into the base line. Subtracting might be what so much minimalism did – removing clutter, melody, and harmony. Randomising was the favoured method of the serialists. And so on.

Precisely analogous methods can be seen in play in the visual arts. These are prompts, no more. The execution can still be good or bad, inspired or dull. But they are useful for anyone involved in creativity who feels they are in a rut or wants to be stretched in new ways.

These methods can then also be used in the work of social design and imagination. Here too you can start with an existing activity, but rather than it being a particular style of landscape painting or musical composition it is a social phenomenon – like care for the elderly, libraries, or the work of a parliament. Then a group or a design can imagine applying these transformations.

Extending an aspect of existing practice means taking it to its logical conclusion: that is, starting with what exists and then taking it further. This is natural for us; for example, extending the idea of diet to other aspects of our lives, such as how we sleep or what culture we consume (the notion of dietetics). Or we could extend the idea of a museum to encompass city squares or special zones in municipal offices.

Grafting (or combining) involves taking an idea from another field. What if galleries included rooms for sleeping in, or childcare? Most innovation involves combinations of various kinds, like the iPod which combined earlier generations of music devices with the streaming concepts pioneered by Napster, the music compression methods (mpeg) pioneered by Germany, and the manufacturing methods of Foxconn.

A more radical approach is to use **inversion**. A classic example is the way in which microcredit turned poor farmers into bankers or the maker movement which transformed consumers of things into makers of objects.

Addition and **subtraction** are also useful: many traditions in the arts involve both. Baroque music and architecture added flourishes, grace notes, and decorations. Modernism took them away, ending up with minimalist clarity, and at the extreme Rauschenberg's *White Spaces* and John Cage's *4'33*. We can reimagine the library or the family doctor in similar ways if we wish to.

Randomness is a way of throwing in surprise: whether to choose words for a poem, notes for a composition, or to throw paint onto a canvas.

These tools generate ideas quickly – taking a field, a product, or function (which could be rural transport, the management of trees, or early childhood education) and then exploring the possibility space by thinking through how extension, inversion, and grafting might work.

This is only the start and a means to get a bigger menu of imaginative options. The next stage involves merging or combining different elements. This is what Samuel Taylor Coleridge called 'esemplastic power', the ability to shape disparate things into one, to take combinations and make a new whole.[67]

So here are examples where methods more obviously familiar from the arts can be applied to quicken imagination in relation to society. Very few of them are used in practice in fields like government or business. But they could be and in these cases the artist isn't acting as a prophet or designer themselves – but rather as an example or a prompt, modelling methods that could become more widespread, a new vernacular.

Collaborative Speculation: Artists Working with Others

To make the most of these tools, architects and artists need to work with others – learning from people who may know more about the materials of social life: teachers, doctors, community workers on the one hand; scientists and technologists on the other. Artists may not be well-suited to designing or describing a future welfare state, family, or city. But they are essential as part of any project that wants to do this, helping to turn abstract ideas into pictures, stories, or metaphors.

Indeed, any serious attempt to speculate about future possibilities has to mobilise all of the senses. Often, we can more easily imagine possible futures if we see or touch something, even if it is more a nudge or a prompt to open up rather than a detailed proposal.

I've been involved in commissioning many works of speculative fiction and speculative design, from possible foods of the future to immersive landscapes, and have come away convinced of the value of using the arts of all kinds to enrich social imagination: seeing, smelling, tasting, and feeling, as well as thinking.[68] I'm also convinced that we need more of this to rekindle a sense that the world can be shaped, and is not fixed. Most of the interesting projects trying to crystallise positive future possibilities have a strong arts dimension.[69] But the role of the artist in these projects is to be a partner and a collaborator, not a god: prodding, nudging, and sometimes shocking us sideways on.

This spirit informs the methods of speculative design. Anthony Dunne and Fiona Raby of the Royal College of Art described it in this way: 'Design today is concerned primarily with commercial and marketing activities but it could operate on a more intellectual level. It could place new technological developments within imaginary but believable everyday situations that would allow us to debate the implications of different technological futures before they happen.'[70] This may involve designing an object that doesn't, wouldn't, or couldn't exist in the real world. The aim is to initiate a discussion around whether that object would be desirable, or playfully thinking ahead to how, for example, assistive technologies in the home or smart cities could evolve, showing how they might be experienced and what could go wrong. A related method is what Bastien Kerspern has called design fiction, a method that relies on 'fictitious artefacts': again, the aim is to be provocative rather than prescriptive.[71]

Some do try to be more rigorous – to ensure that works of science fiction accord with the laws of physics, or that the kind of future economy found in books like Kim Stanley Robinson's descriptions of Mars make sense to economists. But there seems to be a trade-off. Either you can try to introduce rigour and realism, and so be useful from the point of view of design, or you can worry less about them and attend more to the lateral logic of art: it's hard to do both well.[72]

Liberating Time for Creativity and Exploring Our Own Tangents

All of the methods described in the last few sections are becoming more easily accessible, in part thanks to a democratisation of the means of production and distribution. But there is also another vital factor in play: time. We will soon have time for far more people to be consciously involved in shaping their societies as well as their lives, rather than taking its systems and structures as a given.

Art was once an activity for the privileged few. Every society had its singers, dancers, and carvers. But the work of fine art, composition, playwriting, or filmmaking requires a long preparation, which is why academies and conservatories grew up to provide space for the acquisition of profound skills, which was expected to take many years. Yet the deep professionalisation of the arts grew in tandem with its democratisation, including mass-scale participation in amateur music or theatre, that was, during some periods, actively promoted by the state.

Photography was perhaps the first truly democratic modern medium thanks to Kodak and cheap cameras, allowing anyone to document their lives and learn to see in self-conscious ways. But the digital explosion took this much further as every phone could picture and record and every computer became a tool for editing, mashing, mixing, and playing. Quantity is not always a precursor for quality, and the jury is still out as to whether vastly expanded access to the means of cultural production has vastly expanded the number of Leonardos and Beethovens. Perhaps the very ease of access has encouraged people to bypass the rigour and discipline of a traditional artistic apprenticeship that was so vital in turning the raw material of genius into recognisably brilliant works.

But what is not in doubt is the prospect that lies ahead of an unprecedented abundance of time which could be used for creativity. Two centuries ago, people on average worked around sixty hours a week in the UK, and more in many other countries. This number has fallen steadily to not much more than thirty hours (and below in a few countries, such as the Netherlands where the figure is now twenty-nine). A more productive economy should in principle allow people to achieve a similar standard of living while further reducing working hours, and many countries are already discussing the option of four-day weeks.

Meanwhile life expectancy continues to rise, going up faster than retirement ages. Current life expectancy sits around eighty in the UK (seventy-eight for men and eighty-three for women), and over eighty-four in Japan. For some, this freed-up time is a matter of choice; for others a matter of necessity (the result of unemployment or forced early retirement).

But the net result is a huge, and growing, quantity of surplus hours that could in principle be used for anything: playing golf, watching films, gardening, hobbies, volunteering, mentoring, or doing nothing. The question of how to organise that time is set to be one of the great challenges of our century, a parallel to our challenge of learning to live with less resources use and smaller carbon emissions.

So how might we organise that time? Will democracy become ever more active and engaged? Will neighbourhoods set up many more allotments and community gardens? Will schools as a matter of course make use of older volunteers? Will new currencies be used to reward these older workers – in the way that timebanks already do on a small scale?

For the arts, this is both an opportunity and a subject. The opportunity is to train many more people in the specialised skills of creation, and in particular to help many more children learn these skills early, when their minds are most open, in recognition that later in life they may return to them.

But this is also a topic to explore. What would a society look like where many more are living a life of relative leisure and abundance? Will we move further towards valuing the hand-made over the manufactured, the personal over the standardised? Will we see the curation of things, spaces, and experiences as a more generalisable skill? Or will more time come to seem like a burden, an endless boring present to be endured?

6 Dialectical Creativity

In the arts, as in society, creativity doesn't move in straight lines. Instead, it moves in dialectical ways – moving between opposites, or, as in Hegel's famous formulation, from thesis through antithesis to a new synthesis (an echo of how male and female come together to create a new child).

Thinking in a dialectical way has become more important than ever as so many have slipped into echo chambers and as social media amplifies the natural human instinct to seek out confirmation of our beliefs. One role for artists is to reinforce these tendencies, acting as cheerleaders or amplifiers of cultural sensibilities. This is what art does as propaganda; serving nationalisms that exaggerate pride, feelings of hurt and victimhood, or arbitrary differences. It is what some political progressive art does too, for example, in the traditions of political folk songs that denounce oppression and also turn complex issues into fairy tales with heroes and villains. It's the tendency of many strands of green arts, and campaigning documentaries that, again, simplify, in order to reinforce feelings of fear or outrage.

They have their place, particularly if entrenched orthodoxies need to be undermined. But if we're to experience more social imagination, it also has to involve hunger for challenge and difference. We need to spend time with people from very different political backgrounds, to empathise with them, and understand what informs their beliefs and world view. And we need to get a feel for how the world actually changes, which is never in straight lines.

From these complex patterns, let me suggest a pattern: that imagination is most useful when it is dialectical rather than linear or deductive. Dialectical thinking can mean many things: the transformation of quantity into quality; the interpenetration of opposites; negation of the negation.[73] But at its core is a dynamic way of thinking that grasps tensions and contradictions rather than wishing them away – a way of thinking that encourages us to think through how each action, or new design, creates its own dynamic and its own new challenges, rather than offering an end-point or a final utopia.

The most potent ideas don't simply go with the flow of change and with the grain, celebrating the direction of history (though there will always be artists willing to glorify the rich and powerful). Nor do they simply attack it, promoting something opposite, a return to a simpler past, or a life of the village or the land (though again many artists have been attracted to this role of acting as a mirror or counterpoint to the dominant tendencies of their times). Instead, the most interesting ideas go both with and against the grain, grasping some of the dynamics of history but also questioning them, challenging them, and suggesting how things could be otherwise.

The examples I gave earlier of artistic engagement with data and AI illustrate this. They are fascinated by technology, sensitive to its brilliance and appeal, but also interested in deconstructing it, pointing out its oddities and perversities and, in so doing, helping us to see how we could make the technology more servant than master.

By grasping the contradictory nature of change, these more dialectical methods open up more possibilities and reassert the scope for societies to bend the future. Real societies are always impure, hybrids of multiple cultures.[74] Overly pure organisations or societies quickly fall apart. And so we need arts that are at ease with complexity and ambiguity too, a spirit helpfully encouraged by the disparate efforts to create theories of metamodernism as a successor to postmodernism.[75]

Saying Goodbye: Elegy and Nostalgia Making Way for Imagination

I've emphasised so far how we imagine and create the new. But to do so, we often need to find good ways to leave the old behind and make space for the new. Here too we can use a dialectical way of thinking. There is no life without death, no spring without autumn.

The arts often grasp this well and they are present always in funerals and memorials, with music, readings, and solemn imageries, on the cusp of mourning and celebration.

Moreover, any process of social or economic change involves loss as well as gain. J. W. Turner's extraordinary painting, *Fighting Temeraire*, captures the emotional ambivalence this involves. His painting shows an ugly small steamboat pulling a beautiful sailing ship into the yard for the last time, where it will be broken up. All that the sailing ship represents – the cultivation of forests, carpentry, ship-building, sailing skills, as well as centuries of history, meaning, hopes, and, yes, dreams – are being broken up. But the painting also shows how this can be done with respect and grace.

A similar task faces us as when we imagine our own era. A good example is moving beyond a fossil-fuel economy. Much of what we have to leave behind is full of meaning. Coal mining is linked to a myriad of associations, meanings, and identities. The car industry that once dominated my home town of Luton sat at the heart of an economy based on carbon, but now represents a past we have to move beyond.

We use dreams to imagine the future. But we also use them to process or make sense of the past – the things we should have done or said, the blockages and traumas, the things we have to say goodbye to.

Something similar happens at a collective level, and we may need rituals to help us say goodbye to organisations and institutions that have served us well: the traditional hospital that no longer fits what we need for health; old jobs; our nineteenth-century forms of democracy; the village churches that no longer have a congregation.

The people involved in innovation at the frontiers can often be dismissive or even contemptuous of the old and the people linked to it, who they see as anachronisms, 'has-beens' and 'past-its'. That may be a necessary emotion when campaigning for change. But once you're winning, you need to change gear and to be graceful in victory: if you don't, you'll find you have many enemies, dreaming ever more intensely of a lost past rather than a possible future.

These processes of collective memory are also slow. The First World War came to be seen as disaster only more than a decade after it had finished, thanks to novels and plays. The full meaning of the Holocaust likewise took several decades to crystallise. Similarly, the scale, significance, and horror of the Cultural Revolution in China took decades to emerge. The arts have an essential role in this work of consolidating our shared memory, making sense of traumas so that we can then move on.

The Anthropocene and the Post-Human Future

The hardest 'goodbye' we may need to say is to our ideal of ourselves. The arts we have inherited saw themselves as deeply humanist. They believed us to be Godlike, at least in our potential. The more the individual spirit could be set free, the more it would thrive. Now we recognise that we do indeed live in an Anthropocene era, a world where humans have reshaped our environment, the geology as well as the biology of the earth. But with this realisation has come a dawning humility. We no longer see humans as innately good – rather recognising that they contain a multitude of different pulls, desires, instincts, and biases. We no longer see our dominion over nature as altogether benign. Indeed, in some green philosophies, encouraged by what we know of prehistory, we verge on self-hatred, believing that humans are uniquely competitive, violent, and destructive, a species doomed to suicide and self-made extinction.

This extraordinary shift in world views poses a challenge for the arts. How should they help us to make sense of a possibly post-human future? How should they help us appreciate, with humility, our smallness in the vastness of the universe, and the contingency of our position amidst a multiplicity of life as well as novel intelligences? How can they help us grasp both the opportunities of post-human futures – how our senses might be amplified, our bodies transformed with prosthetics, our brains linked up to each other – but also the losses that will come too? None of this is easy but this is exactly the space where the arts can explore, perhaps more easily than logical analysis.

There is a subtler job to be done too. It's fascinating to compare our times with the prehistoric art of Lascaux, Altamira, and Chauvet. These present a world in which humans are minor players, rarely represented, if at all, in almost cartoon-like forms, while around them are beautifully portrayed aurochs, mammoths, stags, and horses for which we are at most a minor irritant. Perhaps this is also one kind of future for us to imagine, a return to being bit players. Art can help us imagine what it might be like to be so marginal, perhaps aided by grasping what it is like to be a bat, an ant, a cloud, or a sprawling mycelium right now.

If eighteenth century and nineteenth century romantic imagination was all about the glorification of the human, perhaps what our times need most now is something radically different: a stance that is humble and self-effacing but without sliding into destructive self-hatred; an art that can see the still-unrealised potential of our brains and bodies but without illusions.

7 Combining Order and Chaos in Tangential Imagination

In Schelling's famous work on imagination, he described the work of art as where 'all contradictions are dissolved and all riddles solved'.[76] Now we see things in an opposite way. A great work of art is one whose meanings cannot be contained with any interpretation, whose sense exceeds the sense-making capacity of any viewer or reader. Art contains multitudes.

This evident gap between the work of art and its potential to be grasped or made sense of prompts an analogy in how we think of ourselves or the societies around us: the thought that there is always a big gap between what we are and what we could be, and between what our society is and what it could be. That greater possibility involves growth: a potential not just to contain multitudes, but also to integrate and synthesise them.

Here the arts provide both analogies and prompts. This is oddly most apparent in the art forms that are least representational and furthest away from the image. Music, for instance, often plays with consonance and dissonance. For the last two centuries, rebellion in music repeatedly manifested itself in the form of accentuated dissonance. But there was a dialectical pattern in play since what was heard as dissonance in one generation became consonance in the next, and within the musical piece itself there was, and is, always a need for both repetition and novelty, dissonance and a return to consonance.

For composers, like their equivalents in other art forms, the challenge is not so much how to make war against repetition but rather how to create forms of structure, and repetition, which are hospitable to dissonance. Or as Duke Ellington put it, how to 'sing sweet but put a little dirt in it'. The arts – and avant-gardes – sometimes went astray when they simply ran away from order, and usually at that point lost their audiences too. Now we understand better that the creative challenge is to find a more advanced combination of differentiation and integration, fluidity and structure, chaos and order, clean and dirty.

This is, surely, also a vital metaphor for one ideal of human progress: that we learn over time how to incorporate new kinds of diversity, differentiation, and even anarchy within lives and communities that still have order and meaning, and that combine some repetitive rhythms and themes along with variation. Music and other arts can anticipate this kind of progress – articulating this idea not explicitly but rather in ways that transcend our cognitive limits, and yet still give us a sense of a bigger and richer life.

Something similar may be happening as the arts help us explore the shadows. We all have our own shadows – dark thoughts, desires, and preoccupations. So too does every society have its shadows – the things, activities, or ways of thinking that are disapproved of and pushed to the margins. Even the most rational and scientific societies have shadow worlds of astrology, shamanism, witchcraft, and esoteric religion. These attract highly creative people in all walks of life, giving them a licence to suspend logic and linear thinking.

They are often displaced to marginal places: gatherings in forests, mountains, and deserts. Some become very high profile, like the Burning Man festival and its offshoots, and always the arts are very much present – providing music, dance, painting, and lights in these places which are wilder, less tamed than the mainstream of everyday life. They are an essential part of our social imagination but also matter because one lesson of psychology is that it's unwise to suppress or ignore shadows, which can become malevolent if pushed too far underground. Here too art offers us metaphorical ways to think about the relationship between the wild and the tamed, order and chaos.

Conclusions: Imagination at a Tangent

The heart of my argument is that arts contribute most to social imagination not directly, but at a tangent. They can sometimes help us to picture or describe a future society. But more often they help us through perception rather than prescription; through metaphor rather than blueprint.

The artist in this view contributes best not as a servant of social movements but rather as an agent with one foot inside and one foot outside; discomforting as well as confirming; challenging as well as reinforcing.

But the arts are unable themselves to fill the space they then open up – they cannot become, in Shelley's words, an 'unacknowledged legislator'. They can be ironic, playful, dismantling meaning and pomposity. They can warn and prophesy. They can harmonise with social movements, providing an appropriate soundtrack or a visual accompaniment. Their methods can even prefigure a future society – perhaps one with a shared consciousness and a deep feeling of connection to nature.

Figure 16 Portrait of Wassily Kandinsky, by Gabriele Munter, 1906

But they can't design a plausible future, at least not without many collaborators. They cannot offer a truth about the future and indeed are dangerous when they think they can. Instead, art opens up other truths, and brings to the surface contradiction and tension, in contrast to propaganda which is still and dead. They are at home with resistance, with speaking for freedom; but cannot so easily build.[77]

Shortly after the Russian Revolution, Kandinsky (Figure 16) advocated 'not only the cultivation of abstract forms, but also the cult of abstract objectives'[78]– to the horror of his more obviously political and instrumental peers. There is a place for art that aspires to change the world. But perhaps what we need even more is art that is suggestive, that is not didactic but unashamedly mysterious. Indeed, this is what art is uniquely able to do – seeking out where reason and knowledge can't reach – beyond the sacred, beyond the descriptive, beyond the coded world of technology – and giving us the confidence to be bigger, to escape from the smaller visions of what we can be, the murder of imagination that both pragmatic incrementalism, and overly clever postmodernism, can so easily cause. Perhaps we need this role more than ever; these spaces which can only be explored artistically, at a tangent, not head on.

Jean Gebser titled his book *The Ever-Present Origin*. By this he meant that we should think of origins not just as something at the beginning from which a neat linear flow evolves, but rather as something that can be always with us. This is clearer perhaps in the German word he uses – *Ursprung* – which means 'sprung forth'. So, the creative capacity is something that can spring forth in ever deeper ways, throughout history.

A nice metaphor for this creativity is the famous exercise proposed by the medieval philosopher Nicolas de Cusa. He suggested that we should try to imagine a circle and a straight line or tangent that meets it. As the size of the circle increases its edge approaches the straight line and appears ever less curved, so that, if we imagine the circumference becoming infinite, the straight tangent and the curved circumference become the same, opposites reconciled, a metaphor for thinking beyond limited things towards transcendence, but also a metaphor for how tangents can make us bigger. As we multiply our tangents we move, in other words, closer to truth.

Notes

1. Lola Olufemi, *Experiments in Imagining Otherwise* (London: Hajar Press, 2021), p.7.
2. Through highly selective choices, it's easy to construct narratives that appear to support such links; but it is just as easy to construct very different accounts of the direction, sequencing, and content of causation.
3. This is the metaphor used by David Jubb, formerly of Battersea Arts Centre, in relation to the role of creativity in public life: https://david jubb.blog/2019/09/29/everyday-uses-for-creativity-in-public-life-part-1/.
4. www.theguardian.com/commentisfree/2019/aug/14/glaciers-iceland-coun try-loss-plaque-climate-crisis.
5. Emma Hislop's work on the circular economy goes one step further, suggesting a proto-narrative for more positive ecological futures: https://emmahislop.co.uk/Plaeriet-For-Aether.
6. Assemble, winners of the 2015 Turner Prize, won for a project in Liverpool that involved a local community in refurbishing houses, and then creating a social enterprise from it. The project was practical, serious, and creative. But it was less clear whether the project said much that was very profound about either the problem or the solutions, and, although Assemble's methods were novel for the art world, they were similar to ones used in tens of thousands of community regeneration projects across the world: www.theguardian.com/artanddesign/2015/dec/08/assemble-turner-prize-architects-are-we-artists.
7. My sense is that figures such as Spielberg, Nolan, Beyonce, Jay-Z, or Kanye are not quite in the same category.
8. David. Hopkins, *After Modern Art: 1945–2017* (Oxford: Oxford University Press, 2018), p. 6.
9. Marshall McLuhan, *Understanding Media: The Extensions of Man* (New York: McGraw-Hill, 1964)
10. Rivera was able to sell his work to some of the tycoons of American capitalism despite their unambiguous Marxism. But his ideas caused conflict at the Rockefeller Center. His proposed piece on *Man at the Crossroads*, with, on each side, the *Frontiers of Ethical Evolution* and the *Frontiers of Material Development*, respectively, was destroyed by Nelson Rockefeller, who would have preferred the safer art of Picasso and Matisse.
11. Richter, in a note to himself early in his career, quoted in Susan Tallman, The Master of Unknowing, *New York Review of Books*, May 14 (2020), p. 4.
12. Anyone in any doubt about this should read Frederick Spotts, *Hitler and the Power of Aesthetics* (New York: Overlook Press, 2018).
13. I explore this dynamic in much more detail in my book *Social Innovation: How Societies Find the Power to Change* (Bristol: Policy Press, 2018).

14. Gilles Deleuze, Postscript on the Societies of Control, *October*, 59 (Winter, 1992), 3–7. Original publication Gilles Deleuze, Post-scriptum sur les sociétés de contrôle, *L 'autre journal*, 1, mai (1990).
15. https://hai.stanford.edu/blog/how-ai-and-art-hold-each-other-accountable?
16. Walter Benjamin, *The Work of Art in the Age of Mechanical Reproduction* (London: Penguin, 2008).
17. Pierre Bourdieu, *Distinction: A Social Critique of the Judgement of Taste* (London: Routledge, 2010).
18. I wrote about this in a book I co-authored with Ken Worpole, *Saturday Night or Sunday Morning* (London: Comedia, 1986).
19. For a book on a good example of this, see Fred Forest: https://mitpress.mit .edu/books/fred-forests-utopia.
20. https://voxelarchitects.com/portfolio/b20-museum-decentraland.
21. Mark Fisher, *Capitalist Realism: Is There No Alternative?* (Winchester: O Books, 2009).
22. Massive Attack's recent 'Eutopia' was at least a more serious attempt at a hybrid, serious political analysis, but arguably struggled to work either as music or as analysis.
23. Audrey Lorde, *The Master's Tools Will Never Dismantle the Master's House* (London: Penguin, 2018).
24. Samuel Johnson in his story 'Rasselas' warns otherwise: 'Ye who listen with credulity to the whispers of fancy, and pursue with eagerness the phantoms of hope; who expect that age will perform the promises of youth, and that the deficiencies of the present day will be supplied by the morrow' should take heed of the story. Samuel Johnson, *The History of Rasselas*, 2nd ed. (London: W. Johnston, 1759), vol. 1, pp. 8–9.
25. Karl Marx, *The German Ideology*, vol. 1, part 1 (1845): www.marxists.org/ archive/marx/works/1845/german-ideology/index.htm.
26. See Barbara Hannan, *The Riddle of the World: A Reconsideration of Schopenhauer's Philosophy* (Oxford University Press, 2009).
27. Another good example is *Sanctuary of the Unseen Forest*, a collaboration between Marshmallow Laser Feast, Andres Roberts – co-founder of The Bio-Leadership Project – and artist James Bulley that explores our links to trees. To read more, see www.newscientist.com/article/mg25433860-700-a-city-of-10-billion-speculative-image-paints-a-vision-of-the-future/#ixzz7TQz9Gknv.
28. And more recently of movements of ideas like the 'integral thinking' of Ken Wilber who advocates methods for both growing up and waking up, for example, in Ken Wilber, *The Religion of the Tomorrow* (Boston: Shambhala Publications, 2017), pp. 81–210.
29. Maxine Greene, *Releasing the Imagination: Essays on Education, the Arts, and Social Change.* (San Francisco: Jossey-Bass, 1995), pp. 25–6.
30. There's a vast range of arts projects that are therapeutic, trying to align the inner and outer, personal, spiritual, and ecological, such as the Center for Transformative Media Studies at the California Institute of Integral Studies, https://emergencemagazine.org/, and www.resurgence.org/ (where I used to be an adviser).

31. Jean Gerber, *The Ever-Present Origin* (Athens: Ohio University Press, 1985).
32. Shaun McNiff, *Art as Research: Opportunities and Challenges* (Bristol: Intellect, 2013).
33. Quoted in Louis Menand, *The Free World: Art and Thought in the Cold War* (New York: Farrar, Straus and Giroux, 2021).
34. Daniel L. Schacter, Donna Rose Addis, Demis Hassabis et al., The Future of Memory: Remembering, Imagining, and the Brain, *Neuron*, 76, 4 (2012), 677–94.
35. An intriguing, if very confused, discussion of some of these issues can be found here: http://arsindustrialis.org/anamnesis-and-hypomnesis.
36. Gilbert Simondon's 'associated milieu' is another example, with its characteristic lack of distinction between inside and outside. See the introduction of his book *Du mode d'existence des objets techniques* (Paris: Éditions Aubier-Montaigne, 1958).
37. Eric Shanes, *Constantin Brancusi* (New York: Abbeville Press, 1989), p. 67.
38. See, for example, Paul E. Willis, Common Culture: Symbolic Work at Play in the Everyday Cultures of the Young (Milton Keynes: Open University Press, 1990).
39. The tradition of physical engagement with art works is covered in this recent collection: https://mitpress.mit.edu/books/practicable.
40. See Barbara Ehrenreich's classic *Dancing in the Streets* (London, Granta, 2008).
41. For example, Collective Reality: Experience Togetherness (2016), in collaboration with body>data>space which showed at Nesta's Futurefest, The Litmus Effect – Artist Links (2003), in collaboration with Stanza and Armand Terruli. The project consisted of experiments in sensitivity interactions between humans, data, and space, examining the potential collaborations between public and private space in large cities using interactive technologies and many others.
42. Steven Levy, *Hackers: Heroes of the Computer Revolution* (updated ed.). (New York: Penguin Books, 2001).
43. Shoshanna Zuboff promoted the idea of 'surveillance capitalism' though many had written about it and theorised it over previous decades. Shoshana Zuboff, *The Age of Surveillance Capitalism* (New York: PublicAffairs, 2019).
44. www.theguardian.com/world/2017/jul/25/not-so-fast-despacito-singers-venezuelan-president-nicolas-maduro-stop-using-song
45. https://apnews.com/article/donald-trump-ronald-reagan-hip-hop-and-rap-phil-collins-bruce-springsteen-394ddb622b30a718f1b4621a316a78c3
46. This is explored well in a recent piece by Manjana Milkoreit, Imaginary Politics: Climate Change and Making the Future, *Elementa: Science of the Anthropocene*, 5 (2017), 62: http://doi.org/10.1525/elementa.249.
47. Kim Stanley Robinson interviewed in the Atlantic: www.theatlantic.com/entertainment/archive/2013/04/in-300-years-kim-stanley-robinsons-science-fiction-may-not-be-fiction/274392/

48. Like the UNFCCC's *Momentum for Change* initiative which aims to shine light 'on the most inspiring and transformational mitigation and adaptation activities . . . to strengthen motivation, spur innovation and catalyze further change towards a low-emission, high-resilient future.'

49. Amitav Ghosh, *The Great Derangement: Climate Change and the Unthinkable* (Chicago: The University of Chicago Press, 2016), p. 7.

50. A rare hybrid of social science and science fiction is a collection on writing about the future of economics. William Davies (ed.), *Economic Science Fictions* (London: Goldsmiths Press, 2018). It's a brave experiment, though the writers, perhaps inevitably, are far more at home in dystopia than utopia.

51. Neil Postman, *Amusing Ourselves to Death: Public Discourse in the Age of Show Business*. (New York: Penguin, 1985).

52. For a good recent overview of some of these issues see: P. Törnberg and J. Uitermark, Tweeting Ourselves to Death: The Cultural Logic of Digital Capitalism, *Media, Culture & Society*, October (2021).

53. Maurice Broady, Social Theory in Architectural Design, *Arena: The Architectural Association Journal*, 81 (1966), 149–54.

54. Le Corbusier, *Towards an Architecture* (New York: Frances Lincoln, 2008). First published 1927.

55. www.sciencedirect.com/science/article/abs/pii/S0165032721009125.

56. Quoted in Peter Hall's *Cities of Tomorrow* (Malden,MA: Blackwell Publishers, 1996).

57. See https://archive.ph/20130814093525/http://italiandesignlab.net/archi zoom-associati/.

58. www.artrabbit.com/events/mogadishu-2030.

59. www.artnews.com/art-in-america/aia-reviews/world-architectural-project-mit-press-hashim-sarkis-architecture-politics-1202690156/.

60. www.guggenheim.org/video/questioning-the-future-rem-koolhaas-at-the-guggenheim.

61. It's unclear whether he actually said this, though the idea is expressed in Bertrand Russell, *Education and the Good Life* (New York: Boni and Liveright, 1926), pp. 70–1.

62. Emile Durkheim, *Suicide*, translated by J. A. Spauling and G. Simpson (London, Routledge, 2005).

63. Robert Inglehart, and Christian Welzel, *Modernisation, Cultural Change and Democracy* (New York, Cambridge University Press (2005), pp. 48–76.

64. Gwendolyn Brooks, Paul Robeson, in Elizabeth Alexander (ed.), *The Essential Gwendolyn Brooks* (New York: Library of America, 2005).

65. I've written about this in various books including *Connexity* (1997) and *Big Mind* (2017).

66. www.renaissancenow-cai.org/pdf/Renaissance_Manifesto.pdf.

67. Samuel Taylor Coleridge, *Collected Works*, edited by James Engell and W. Jackson Bater (Princeton, NJ: Princeton University Press, 1985), vol. 7, ch. 10.

68. Many of these were commissioned for successive Futurefest festivals which I initiated at Nesta from 2013 onwards. We also commissioned various writings, like this collection on government futures: www.nesta .org.uk/report/radical-visions-future-government/, and an interesting survey of the interactions of science fiction and innovation: www.nesta .org.uk/report/better-made-up-the-mutual-influence-of-science-fiction-and-innovation/.

69. See, for example, Demos Helsinki's *Untitled*; *The Atlas of the Future*; *Guidebook of Alternative Nows* or their equivalents a generation ago like the *Book of Social Inventions* or the *Open Book of Social Innovation*.

70. Anthony Dunne and Fiona Raby, 'Design for Debate' Online Publication (2008): http://dunneandraby.co.uk/content/bydandr/36/0.

71. www.nesta.org.uk/blog/speculative-design-a-design-niche-or-a-new-tool-for-government-innovation/.

72. William Davies (ed.), *Economic Science Fictions* (London: Goldsmiths Press, 2018).

73. This is Friedrich Engel's famous definition for his 'dialectics of materialism'.

74. I've written about this in many places, including the chapter on Mary Douglas in my recent book *Social Innovation*.

75. https://medium.com/the-abs-tract-organization/missing-metamodernism-5da6b0b35dde is one of a series of essays exploring the many meanings of metamodernism.

76. Friedrich Wilhelm Von Schelling, *System of Transcendental Idealism* (Charlottesville: University Press of Virginia, 1978), p. 226.

77. Nicolas Bourriaud, *Relational Aesthetics* [*Esthetique relationnelle*], translated by S. Pleasance, F. Woods, and M. Copeland (Paris: Les Presses du Réel, 2002).

78. In Wassily Kandinsky, Complete Writings on Art (New York: Da Capo Press, 1994).

Acknowledgements

I am grateful for the very useful comments I've had on this Element from friends and colleagues including Roberto Mangabeira Unger, Wilhelm Krull, Cassie Robinson, Robert Marin of Nuca Studio, and Karina Dobrotvorskaya. The Element follows on from the Untitled project and the piece I wrote to kick it off: www.demoshelsinki.fi/en/julkaisut/the-imaginary-crisis-and-how-we-might-quicken-social-and-public-imagination/. It has been helped by many recent books and projects, including the work of Immy Kaur and Civic Square including department of dreams, Gemma Mortensen and others in the New Constellations programme, and the work of thinkers including Ana Dinerstein, Rob Hopkins, Jenny Anderson, and Keri Facer.

About the Author

Geoff Mulgan is a professor at University College London, and has been involved in the arts as a curator, funder, writer, and policy-maker.

Cambridge Elements ≡

Creativity and Imagination

Anna Abraham
University of Georgia, USA

Anna Abraham, Ph.D., is the E. Paul Torrance Professor at the University of Georgia, USA. Her notable publications include *The Neuroscience of Creativity* (2018, Cambridge University Press) and the edited volume, *The Cambridge Handbook of the Imagination* (2020).

About the Series
Cambridge Elements in Creativity and Imagination publishes original perspectives and insightful reviews of empirical research, methods, theories, or applications in the vast fields of creativity and the imagination. The series is particularly focused on showcasing novel, necessary and neglected perspectives.

Cambridge Elements ⚌

Creativity and Imagination

Elements in the Series

There's No Such Thing as Creativity: How Plato and 20th Century Psychology Have Misled Us
John Baer

Slow Wonder: Letters on Imagination and Education
Peter O'Connor and Claudia Rozas Gómez

Prophets at a Tangent
Geoff Mulgan

A full series listing is available at: www.cambridge.org/ECAI

Printed in the United States
by Baker & Taylor Publisher Services